Hearts and Flowers 2 Mini Coloring Book

40 beautiful designs full of hearts

And flowers for coloring in.

By Artist Dwyanna Stoltzfus

Join the Fun!!

Share your colored pages!!

You are invited to color the pages
From this and all publications by
Dwyanna Stoltzfus. Then scan and post
Your colored creations in
Coloring with Dwyanna
Adult Coloring Group
On facebook
https://web.facebook.com/groups/1519357628356169/?_rdr
Join Coloring with Dwyanna Coloring Group,
And have fun sharing your colored pages
And meeting new coloring friends.
Members of the group will also have access
To free coloring pages.
You are welcome to share your colored pages on
Any social network, make sure to mention the title of
The book and the author/artist name.
Uncolored images may not be shared.

Check out my blog at:

coloringwithdwyanna.blogspot.com

PDF Printable coloring pages available

On Etsy at

https://www.etsy.com/people/dwyannastoltzfus

Follow Dwyanna's art on facebook at

Oodles of Doodles Designs –

Adult Coloring Books by

Dwyanna Stoltzfus

https://web.facebook.com/Oodles-of-Doodles-Designs-Adult-Coloring-
Books-by-

Dwyanna-Stoltzfus-743502922387046/

About:

This is a perfect Valentine's Day book!!

Get ready to color 40 beautiful Valetnine designs by Artist Dwyanna Stoltzfus.

In this adult coloring book you will find 40 beautiful illustrations, printed one per page.

A collection of wonderful images full of flowers and hearts.

You will find lots of flowers, cupcakes, hearts, a butterfly, a teddy bear,

patterns, mandalas and more in this wonderful book.

You can enjoy the beautiful designs in this book for yourself or color them for someone you love.

Your colored page can be given to a loved one for Valentine's Day, Mother's Day,

a birthday, or any day that you want to say "I love you".

You can use this coloring book to help you relax and unwind after a long day.

Or you can use it just for fun. You can color the designs simply or add depth and creativity by shading and highlighting.

Crayons are not recommended for the intricate designs but may be used on some of the pages.

You can also color with fine tip markers, gel pens, and colored pencils.

Enjoy the experience of coloring!!

But most of all relax and have fun!!

Coloring tips:

If you desire to add depth to your coloring you can shade with colored pencils.

Use dark colors around edges and into the peaks. Blend in light colors for the

middle and more open spaces. You can use black to darken areas,

and white to lighten and brighten areas.

Acknowledgments

Thank You to my family for all your support

of my art and this project.

I could not have done it without you!!

Thank You God for the gift and love

Of art and drawing!!

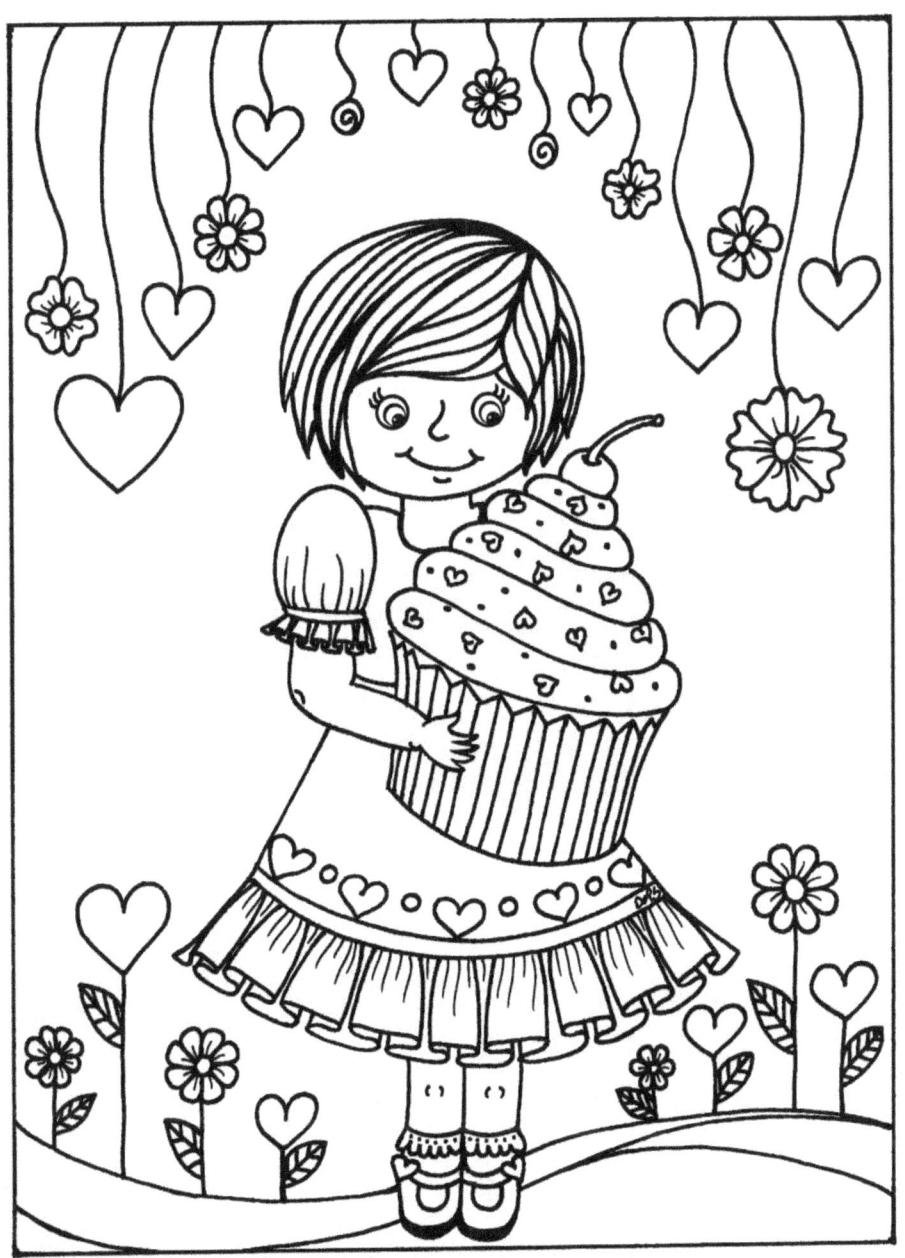

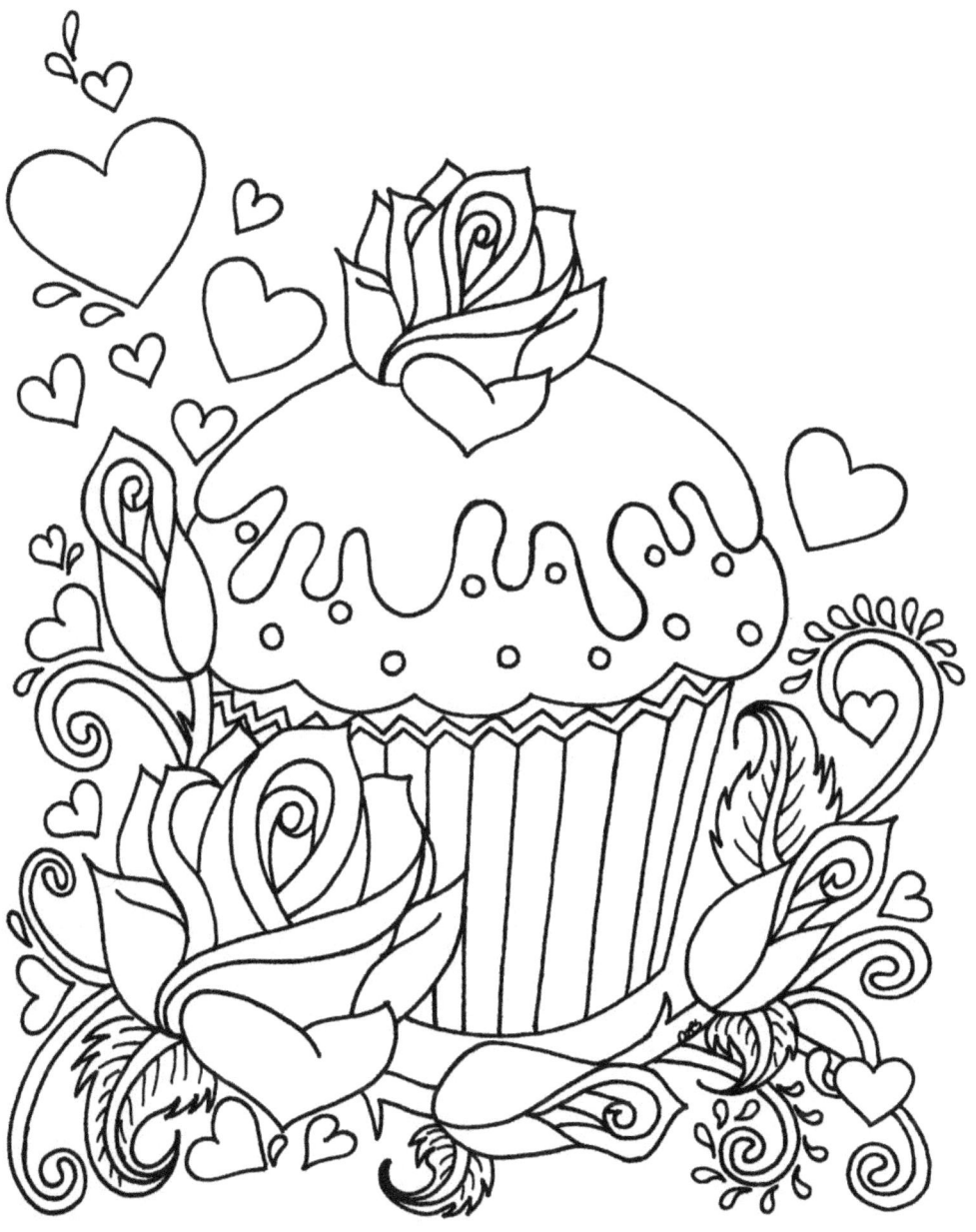

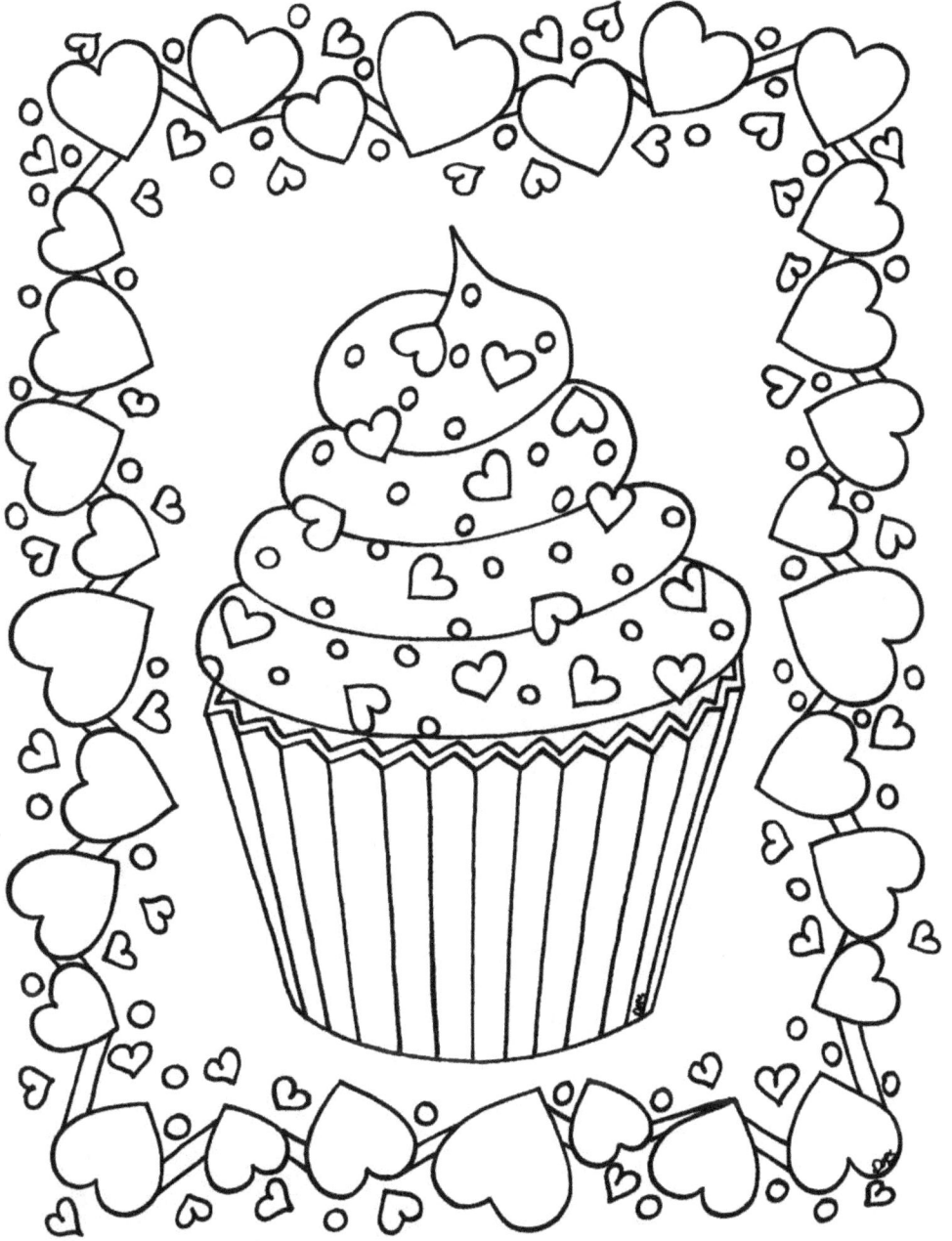

LOVE

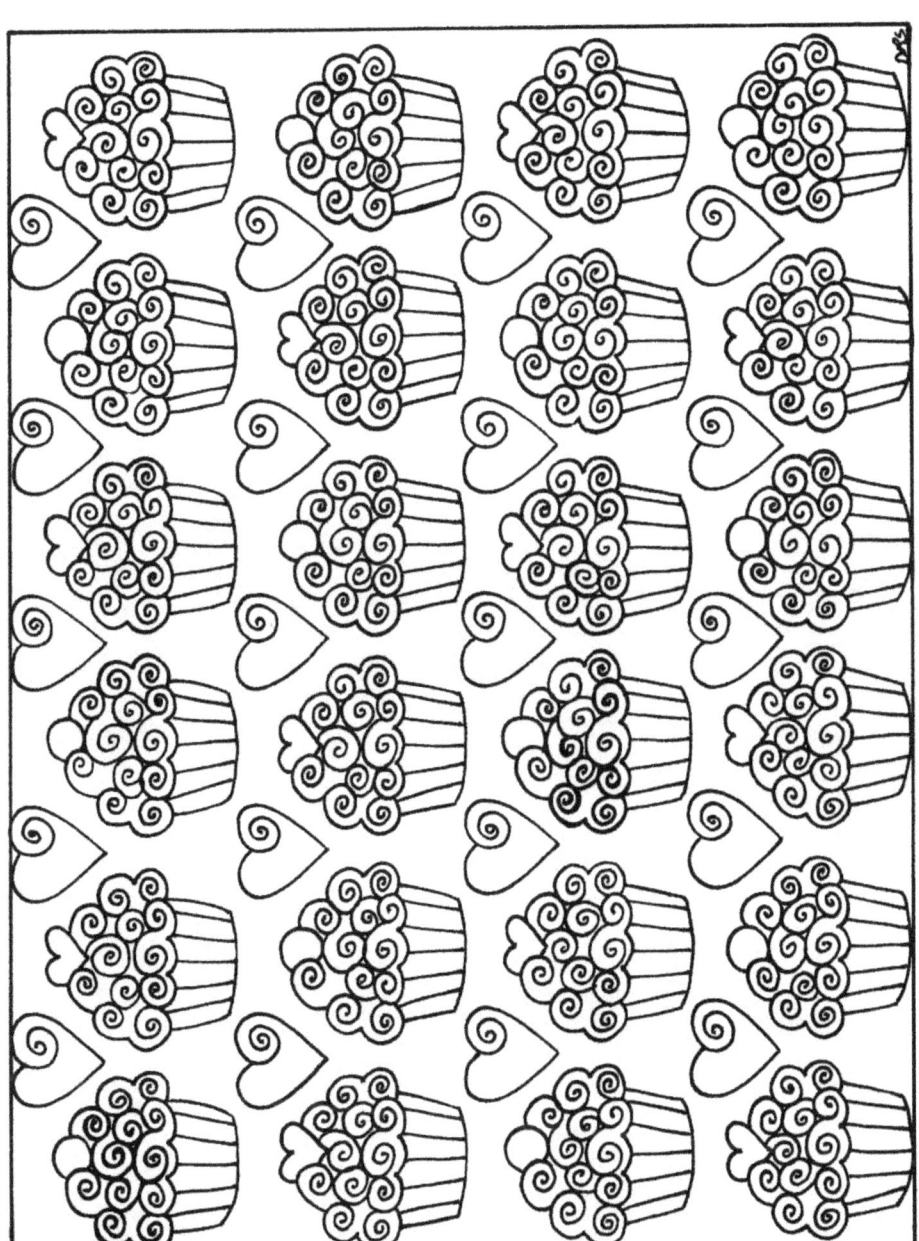

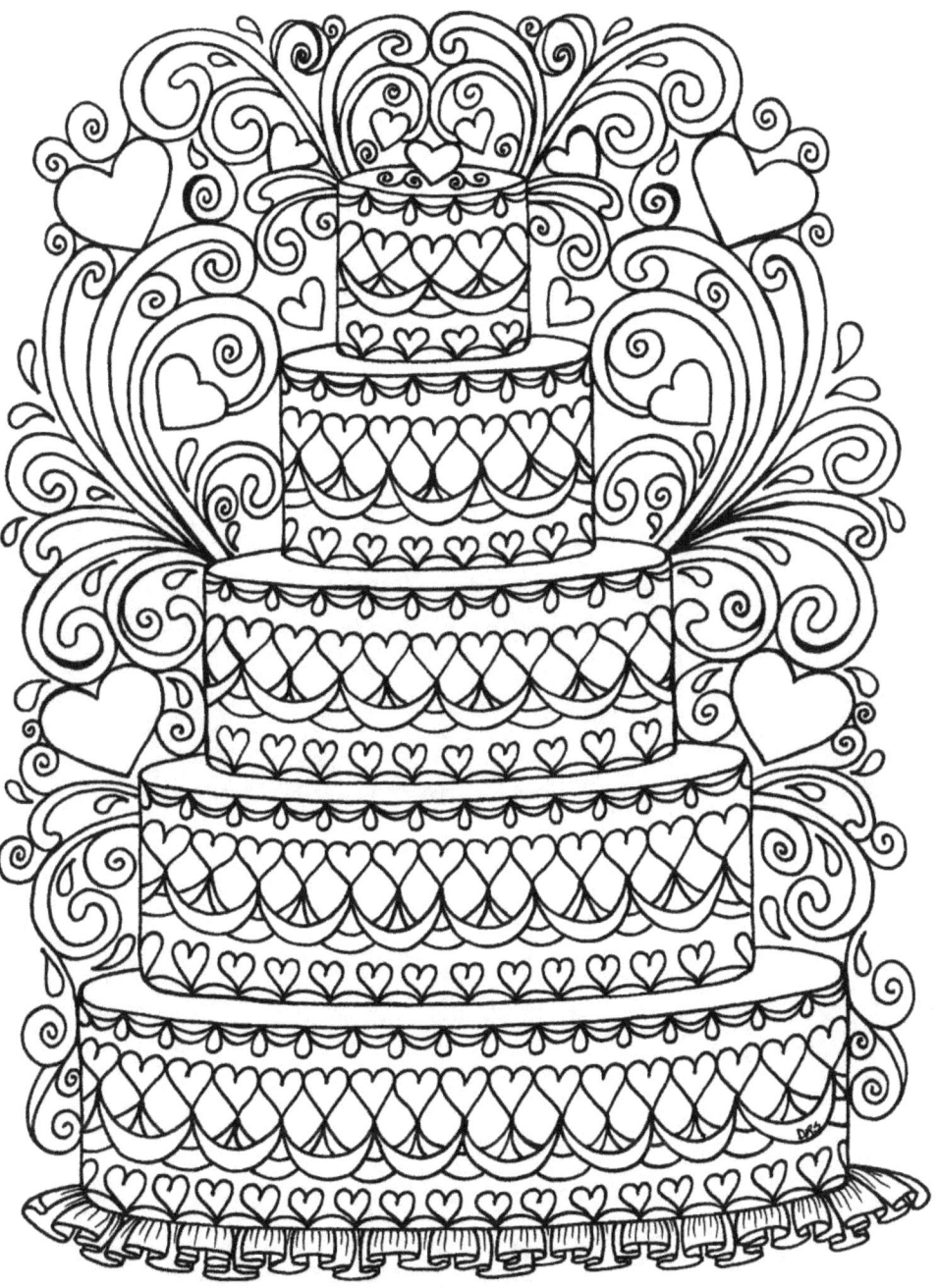

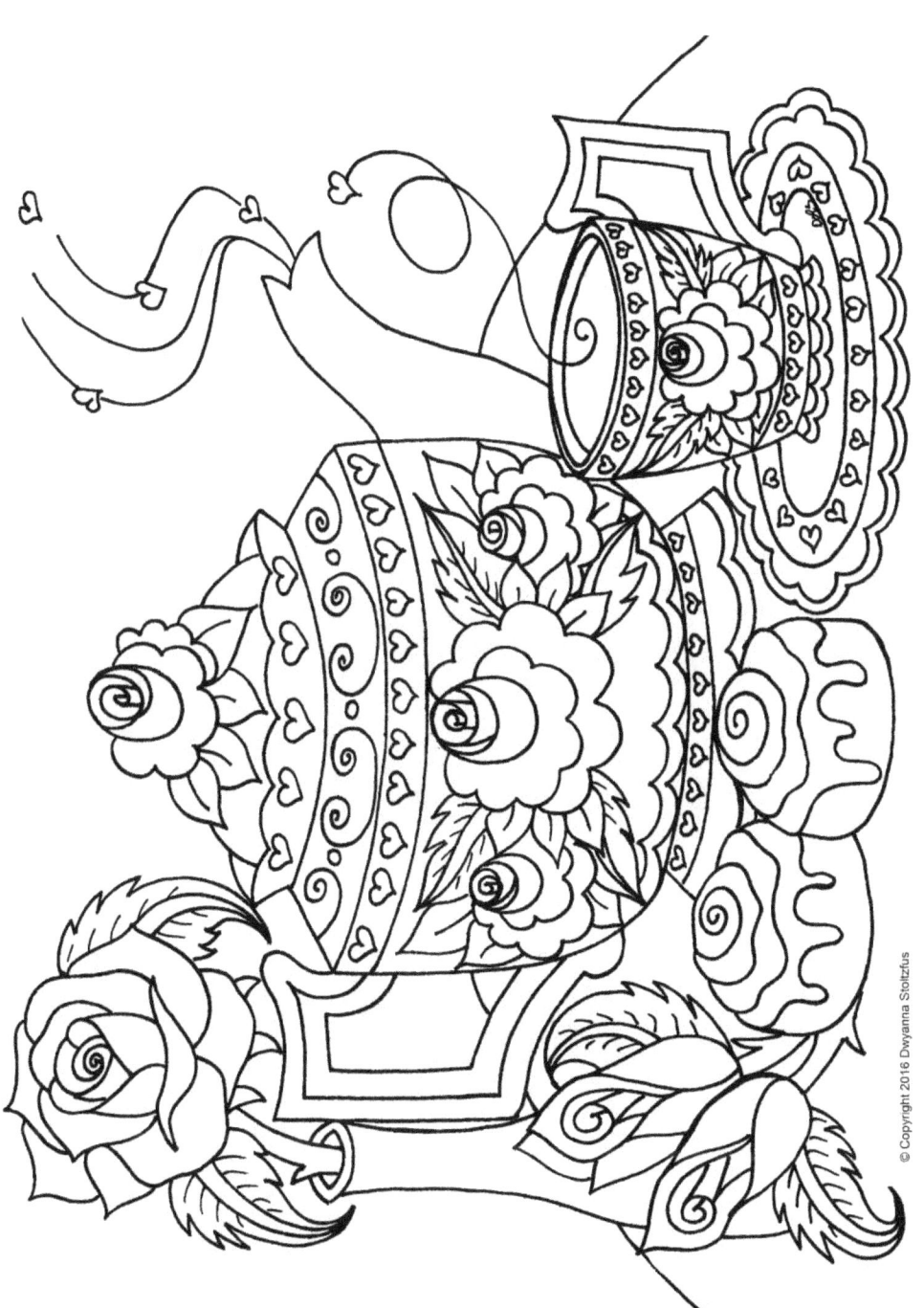

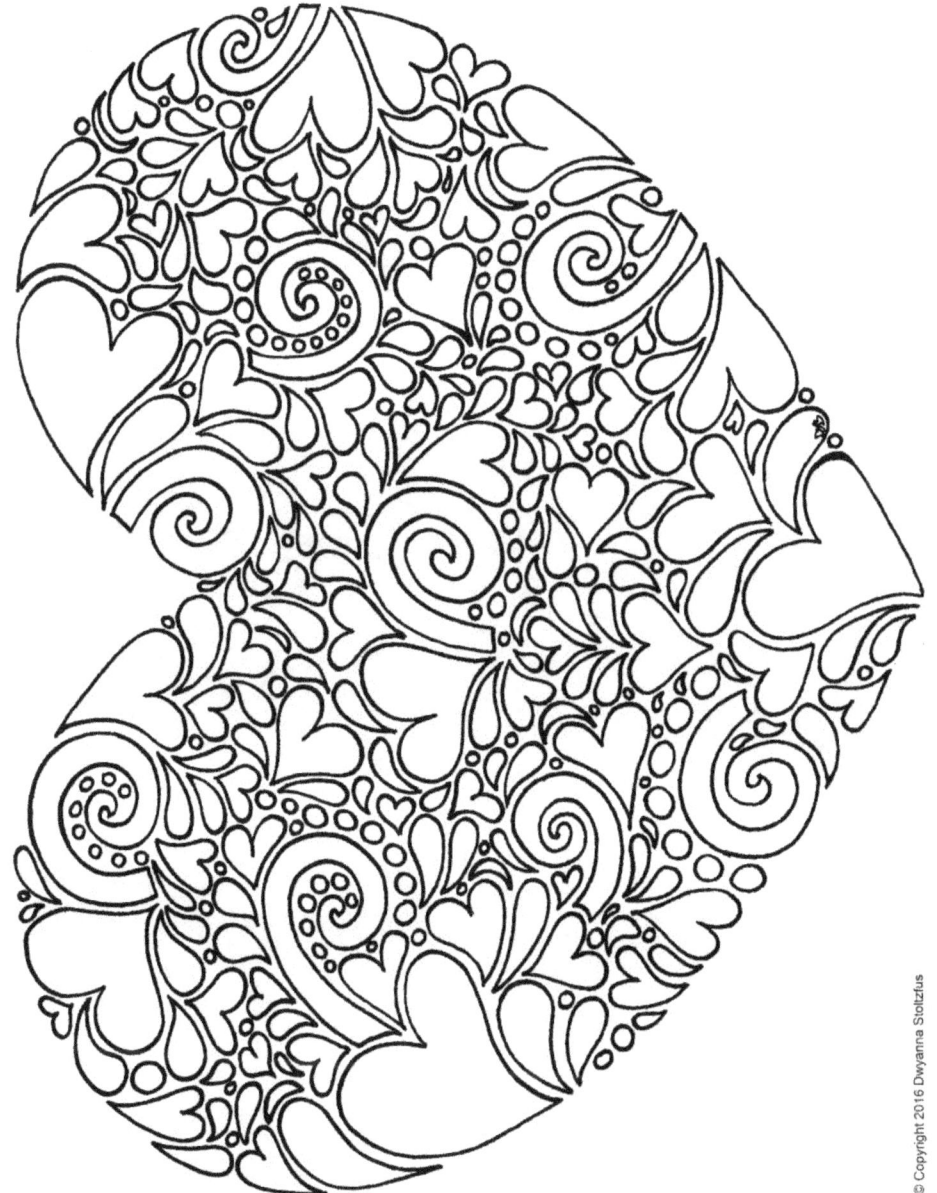

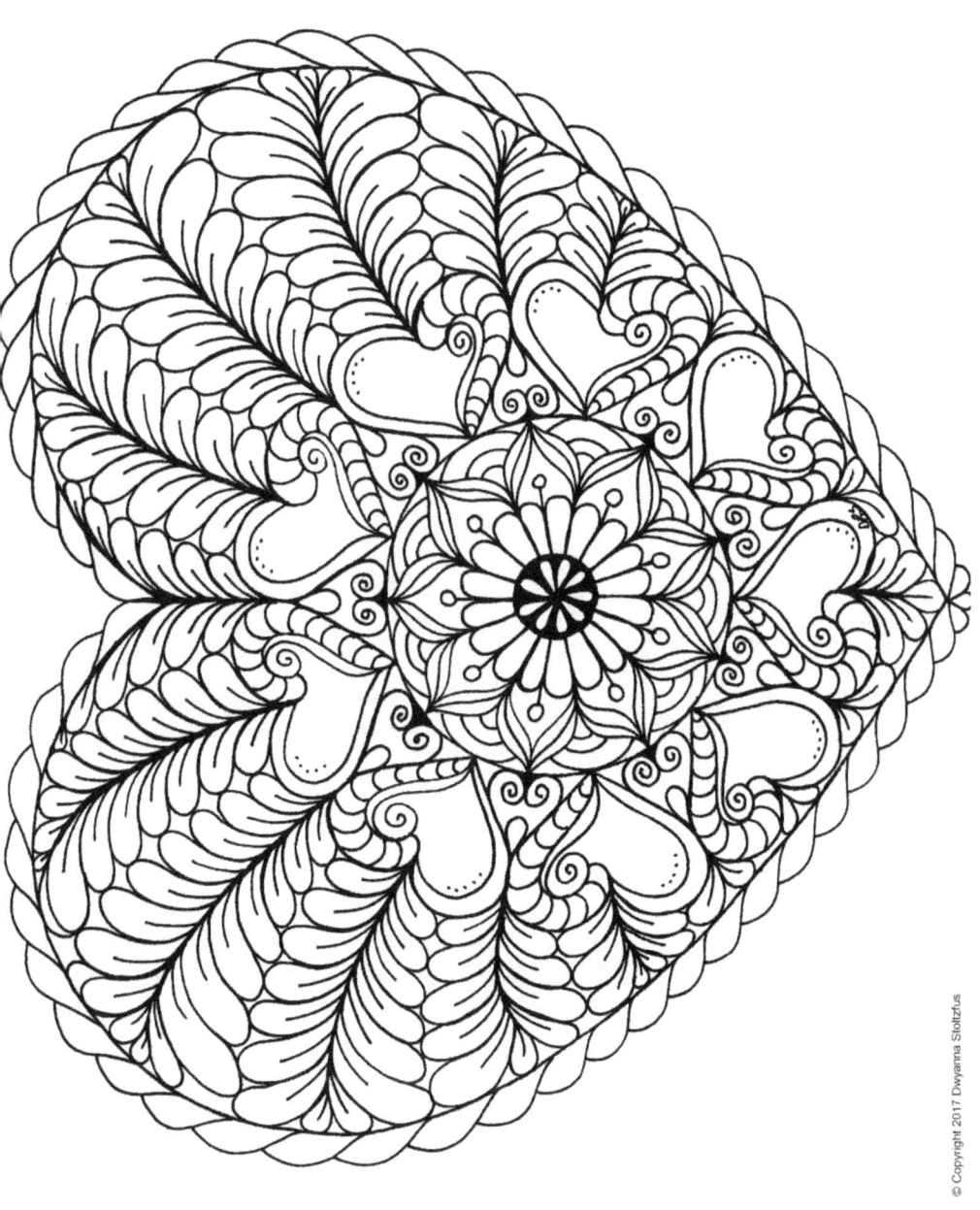

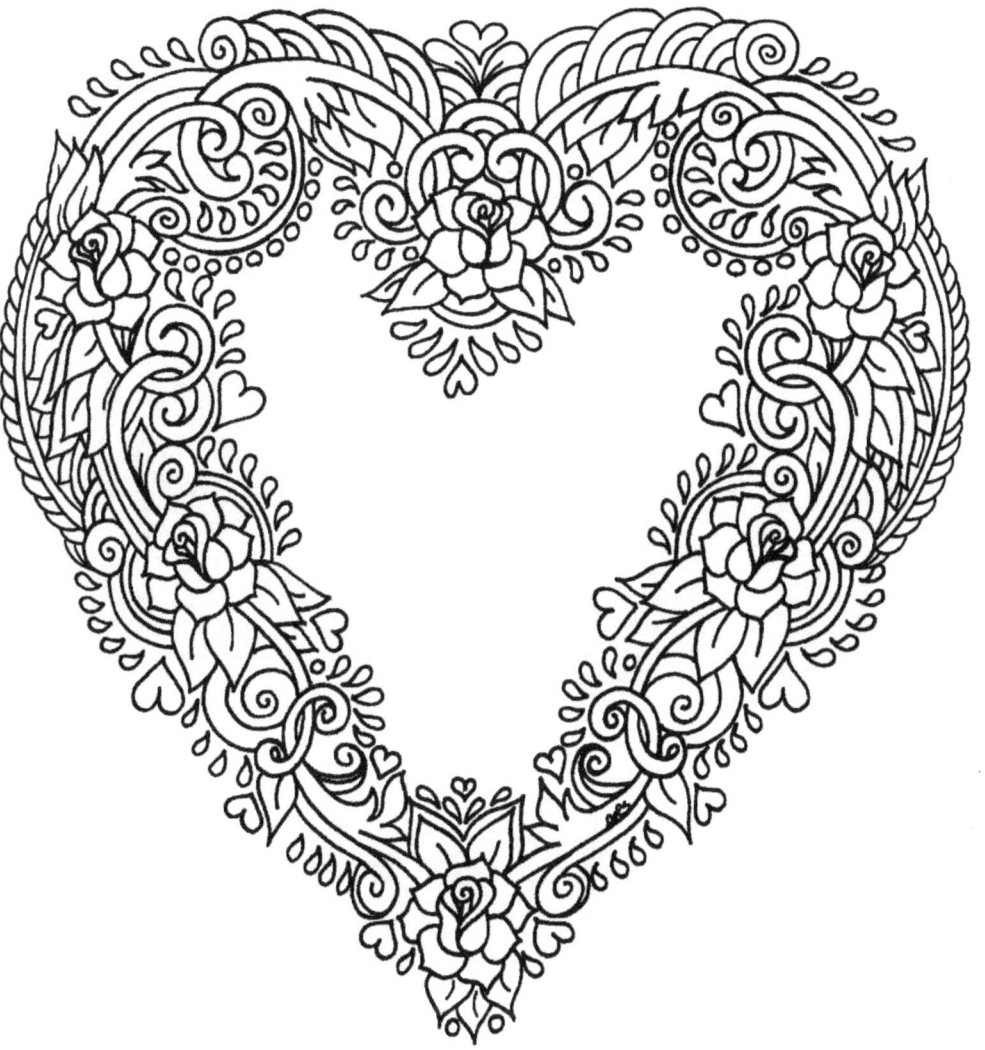

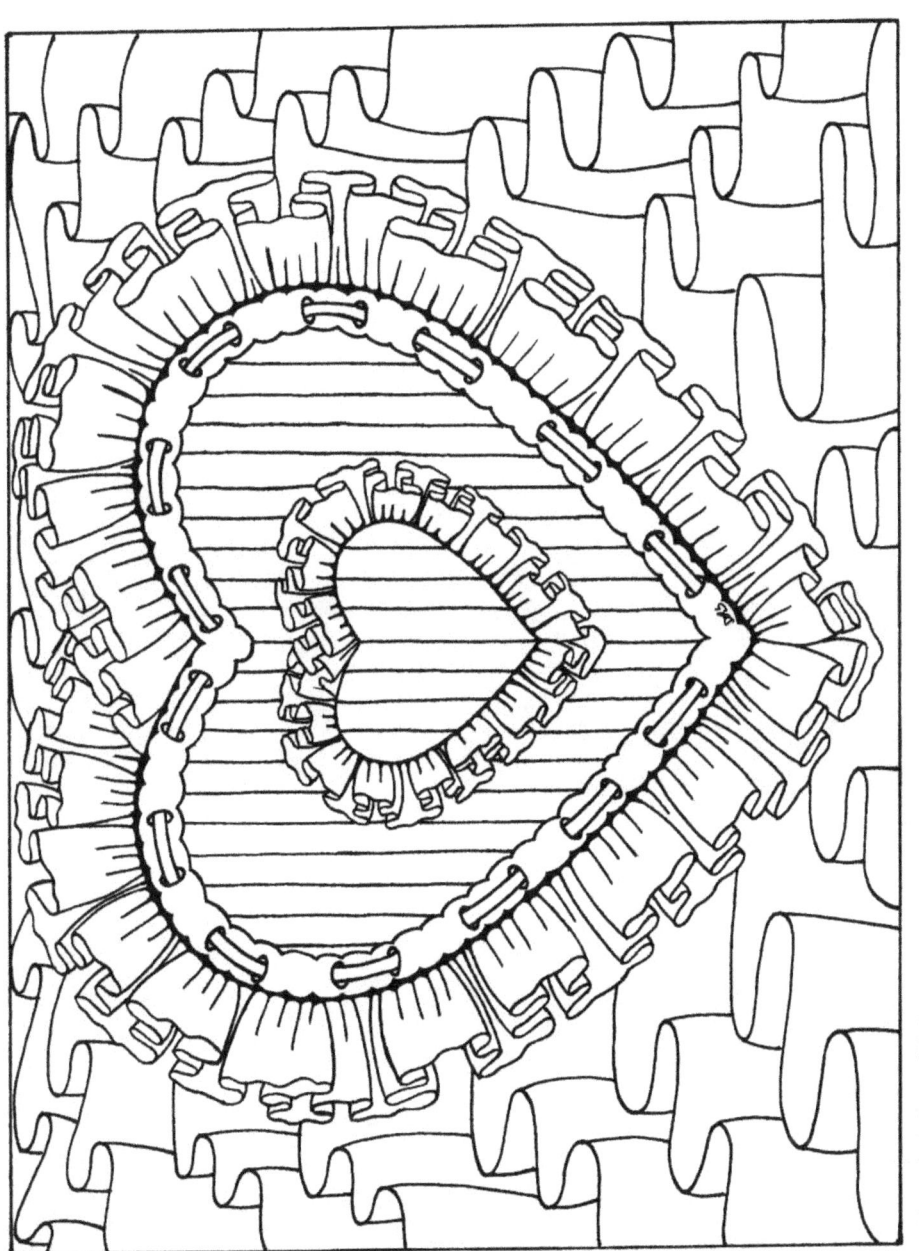

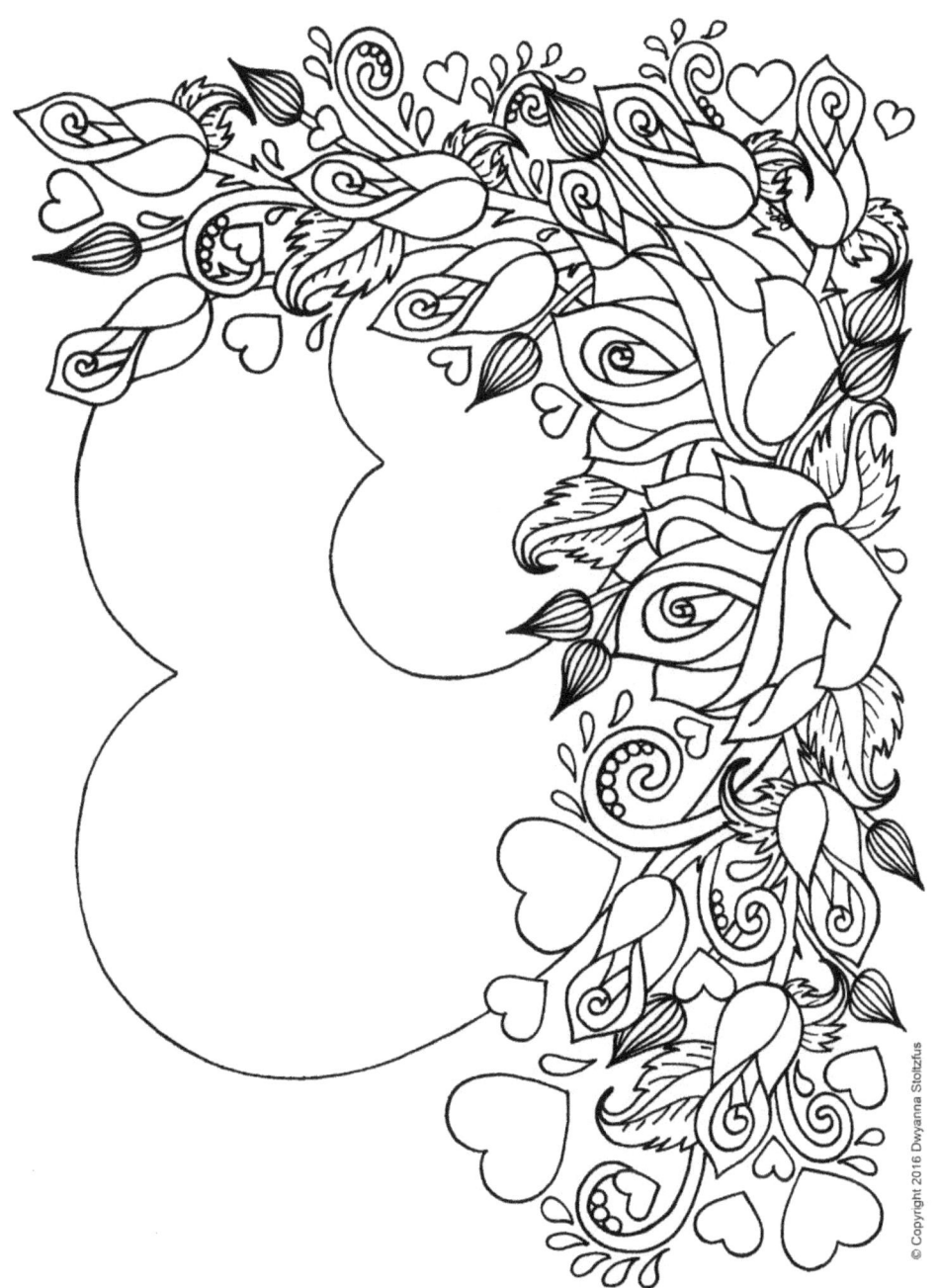

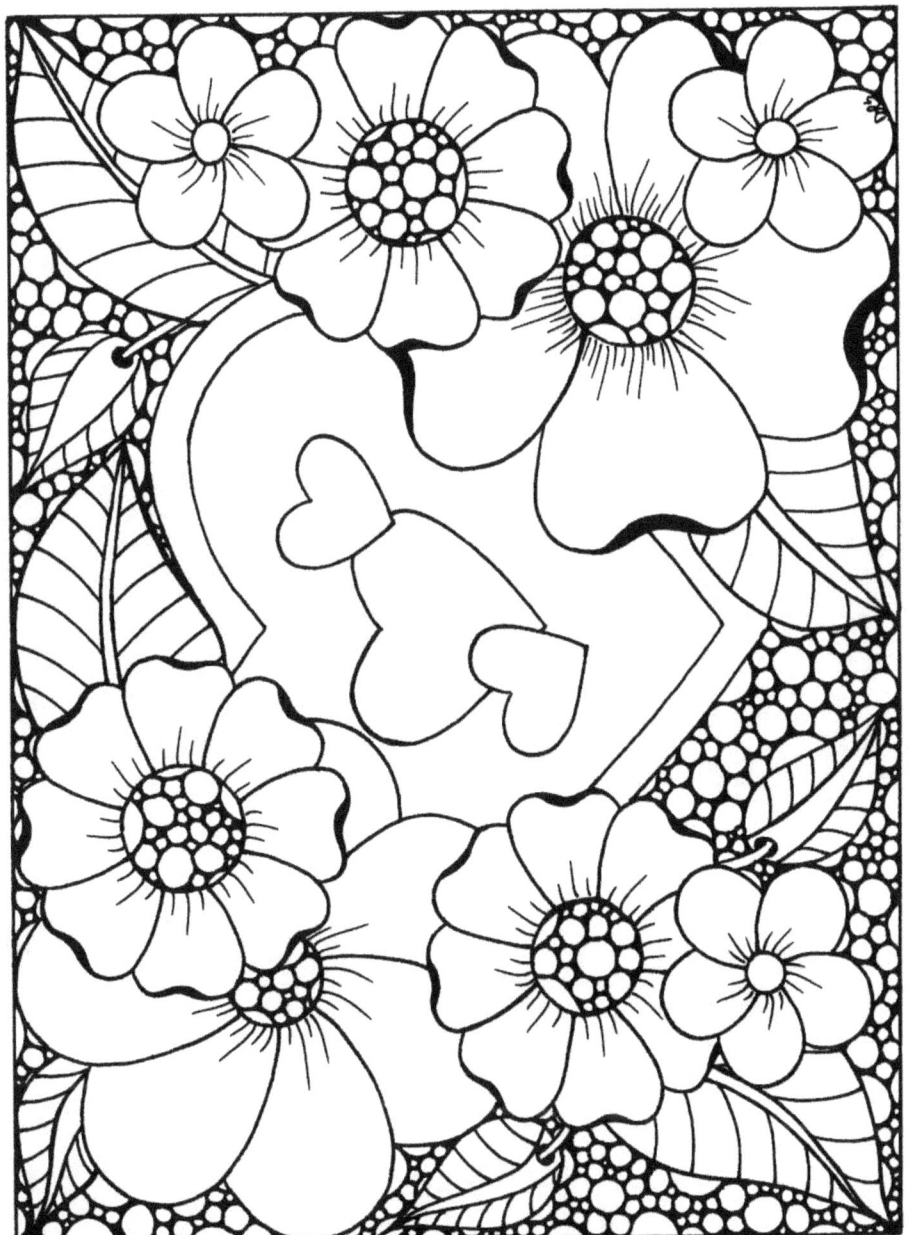

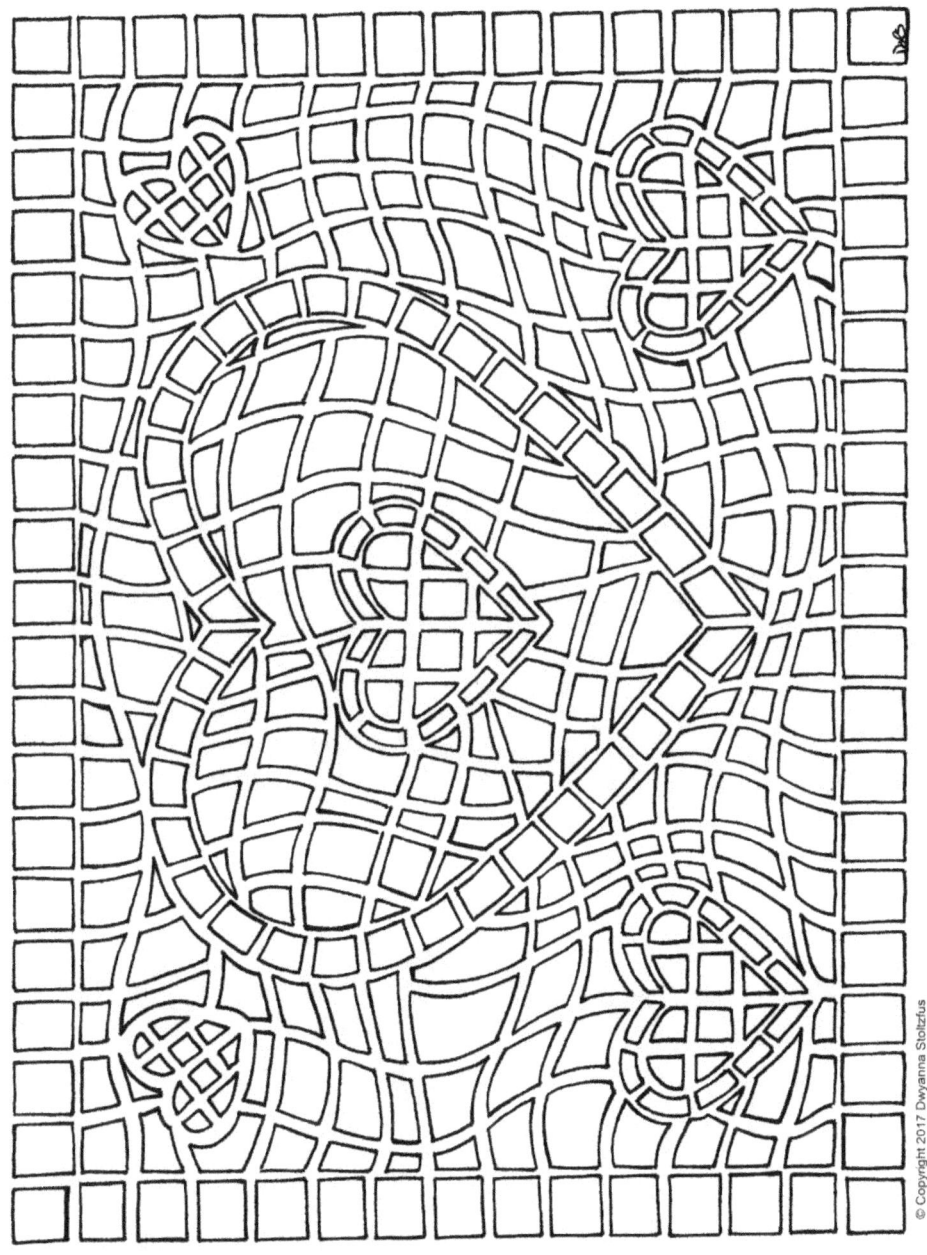

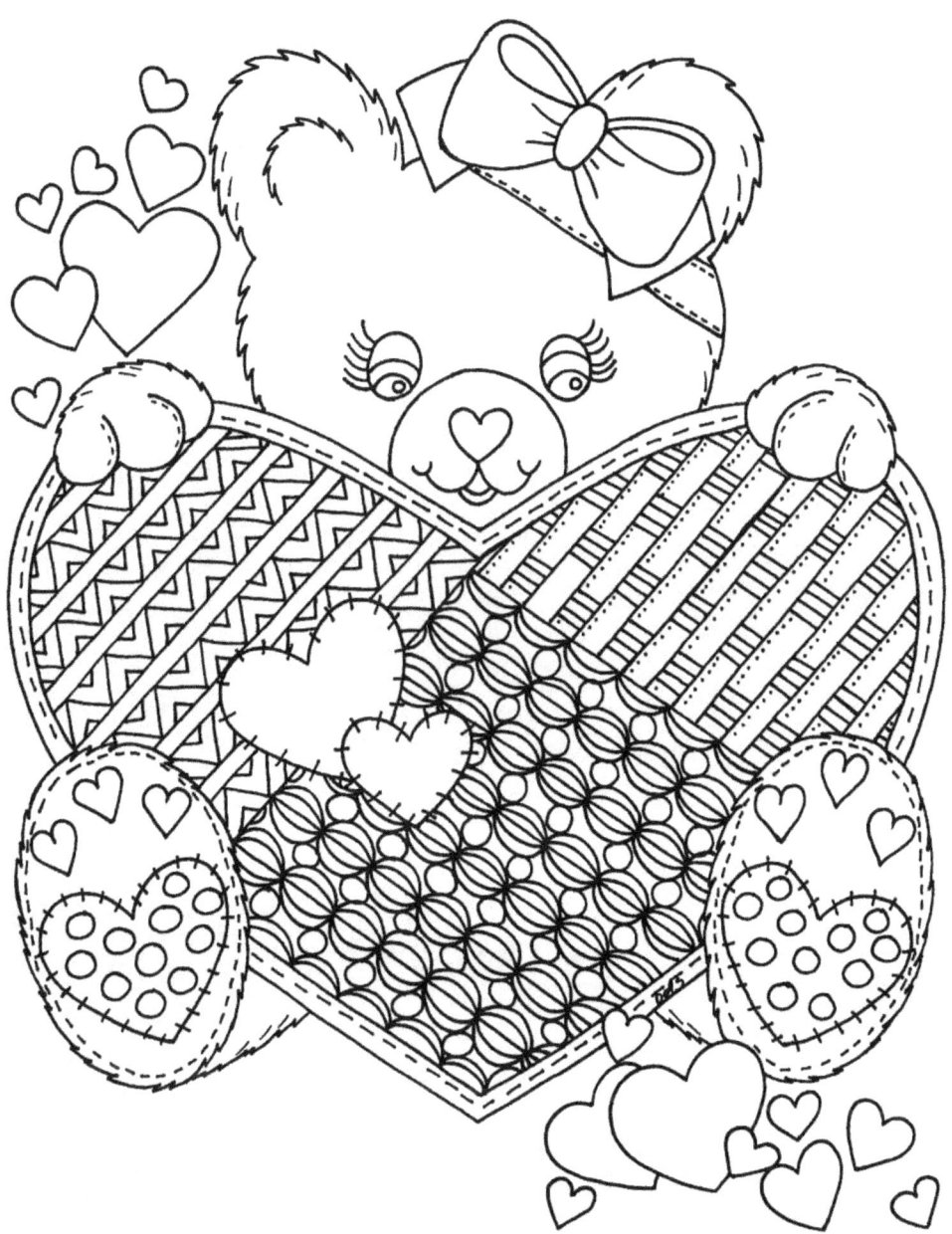

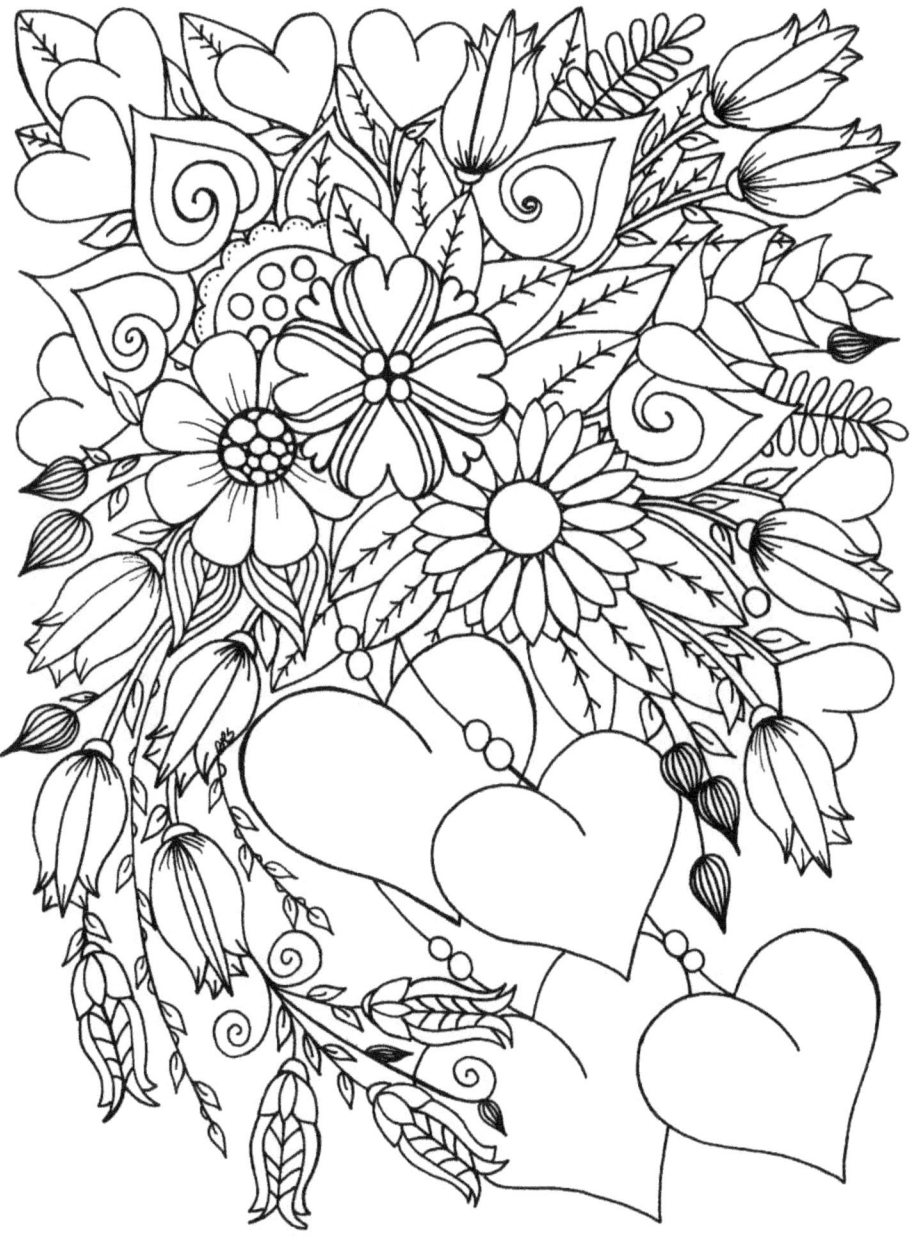

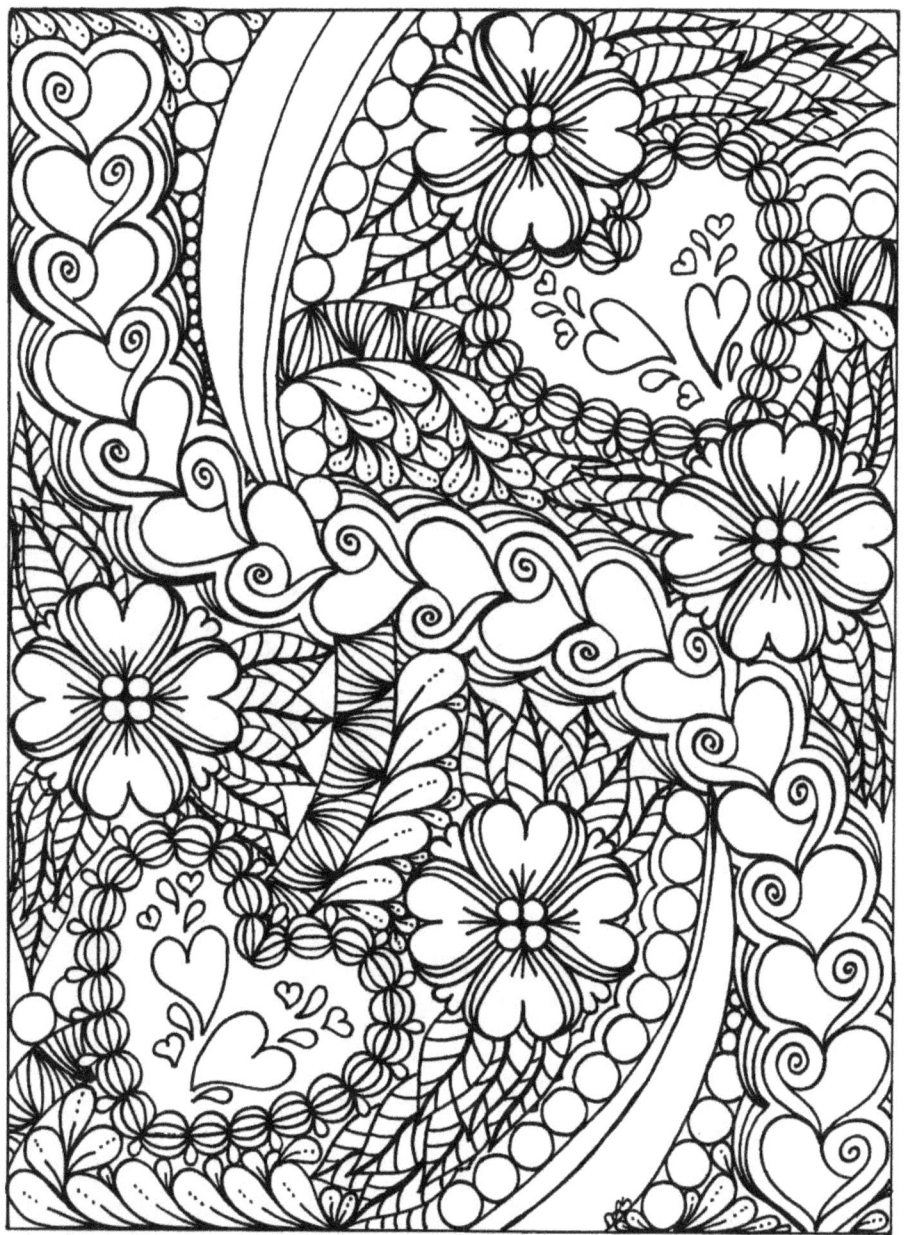

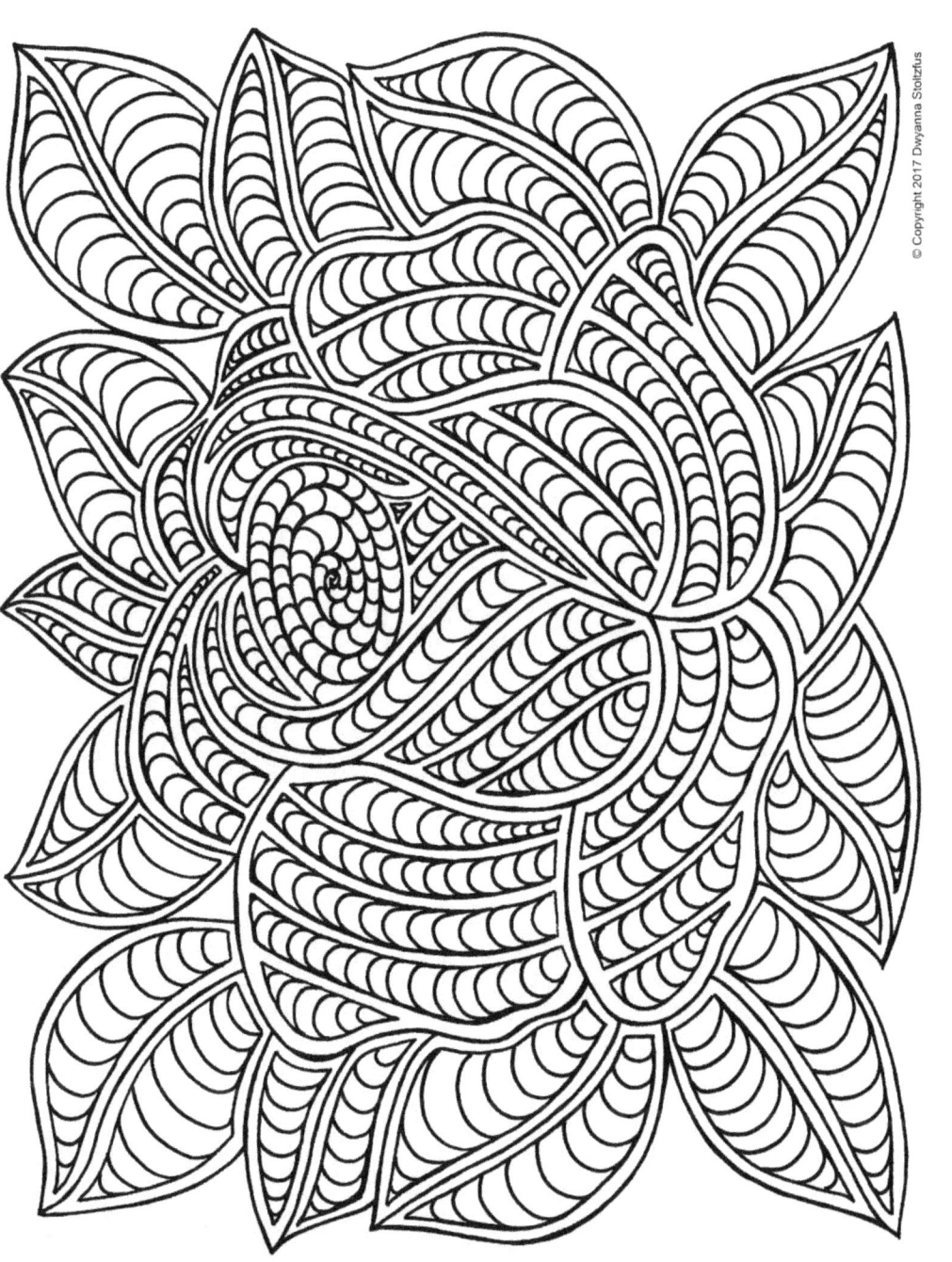

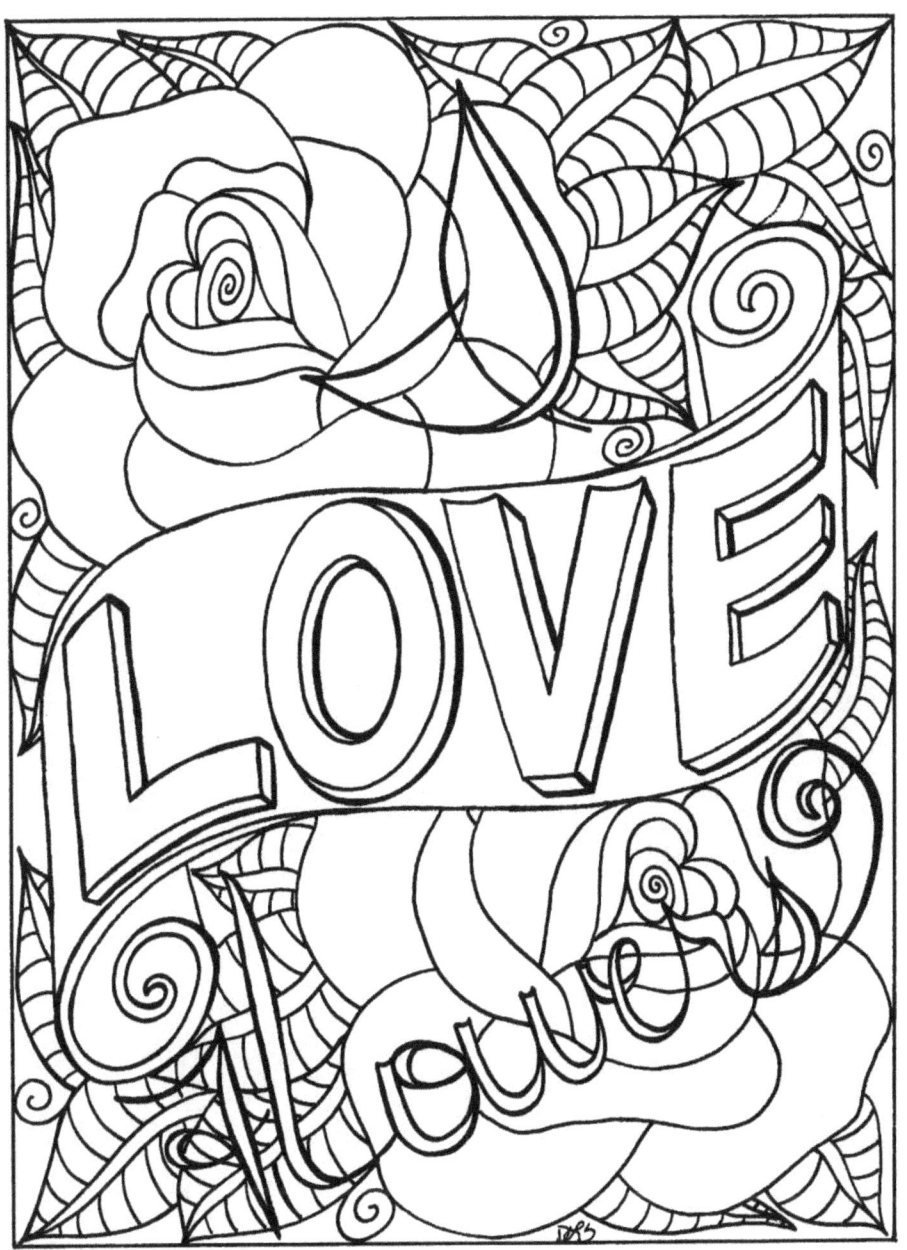

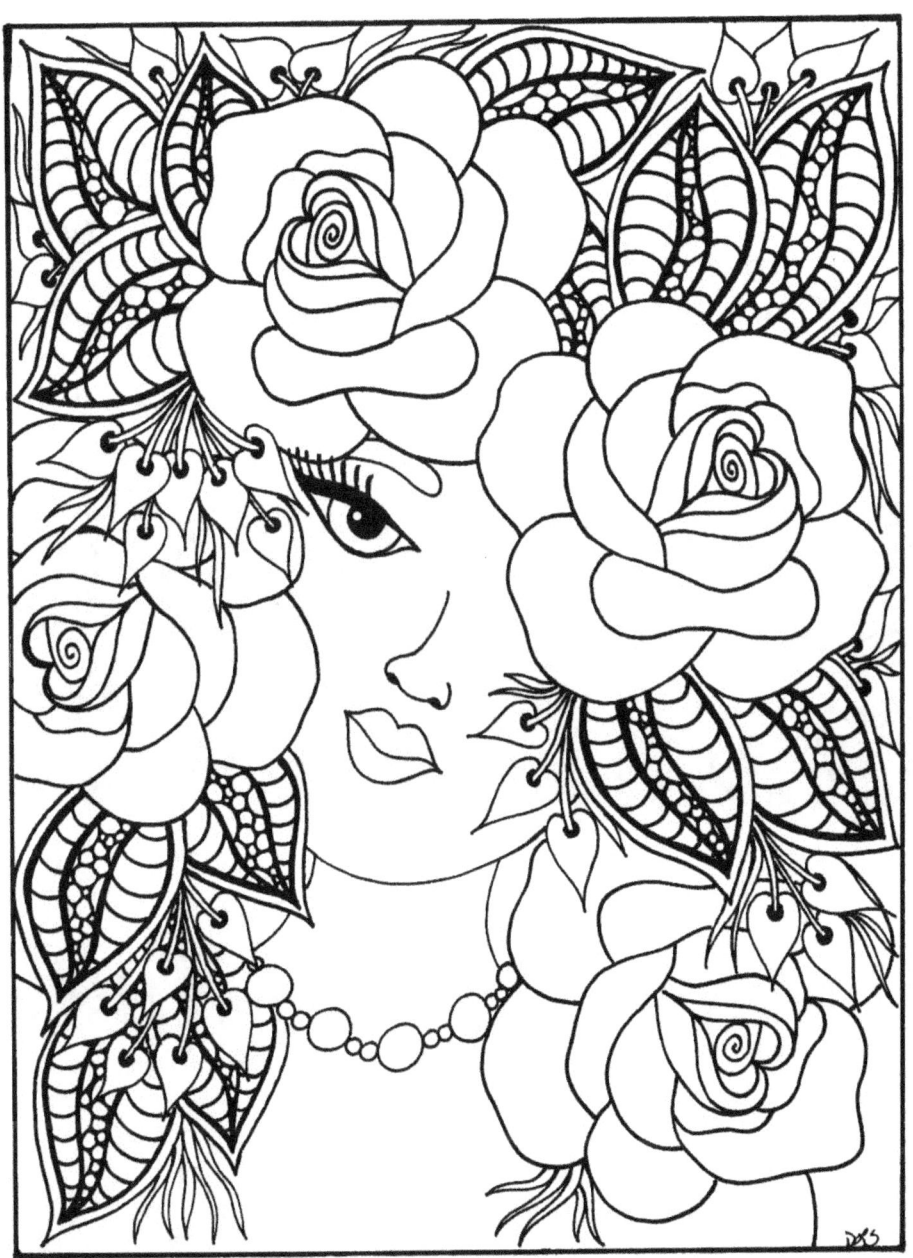

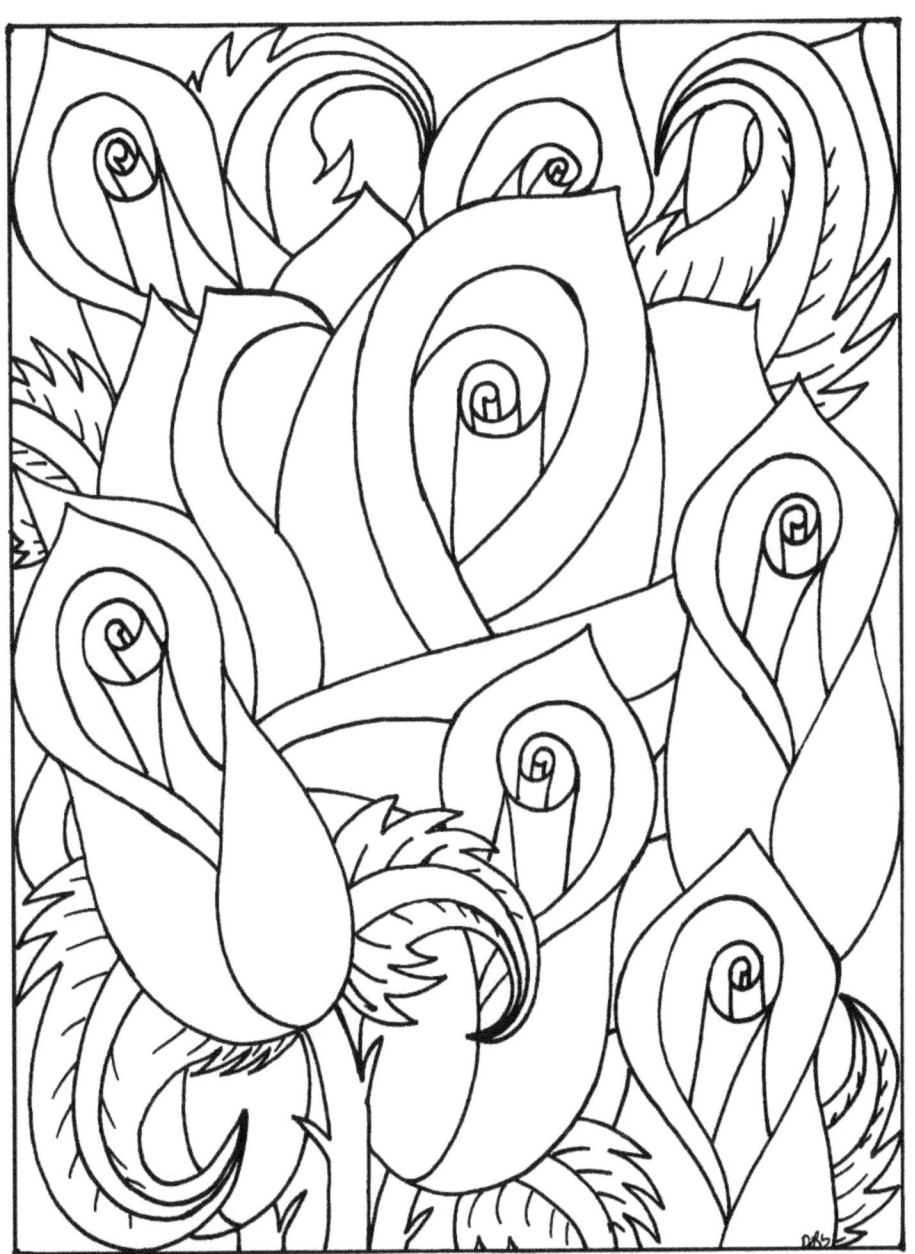

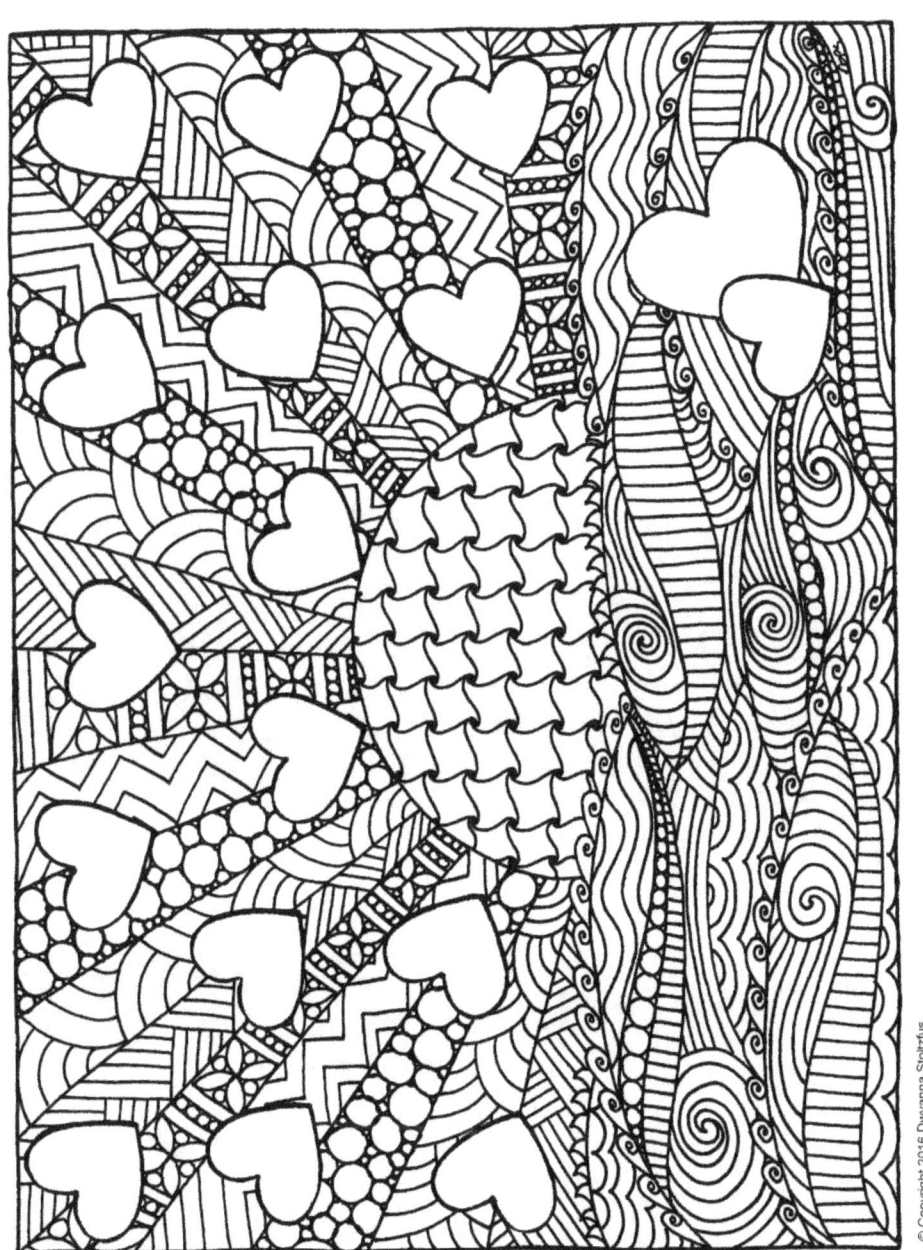

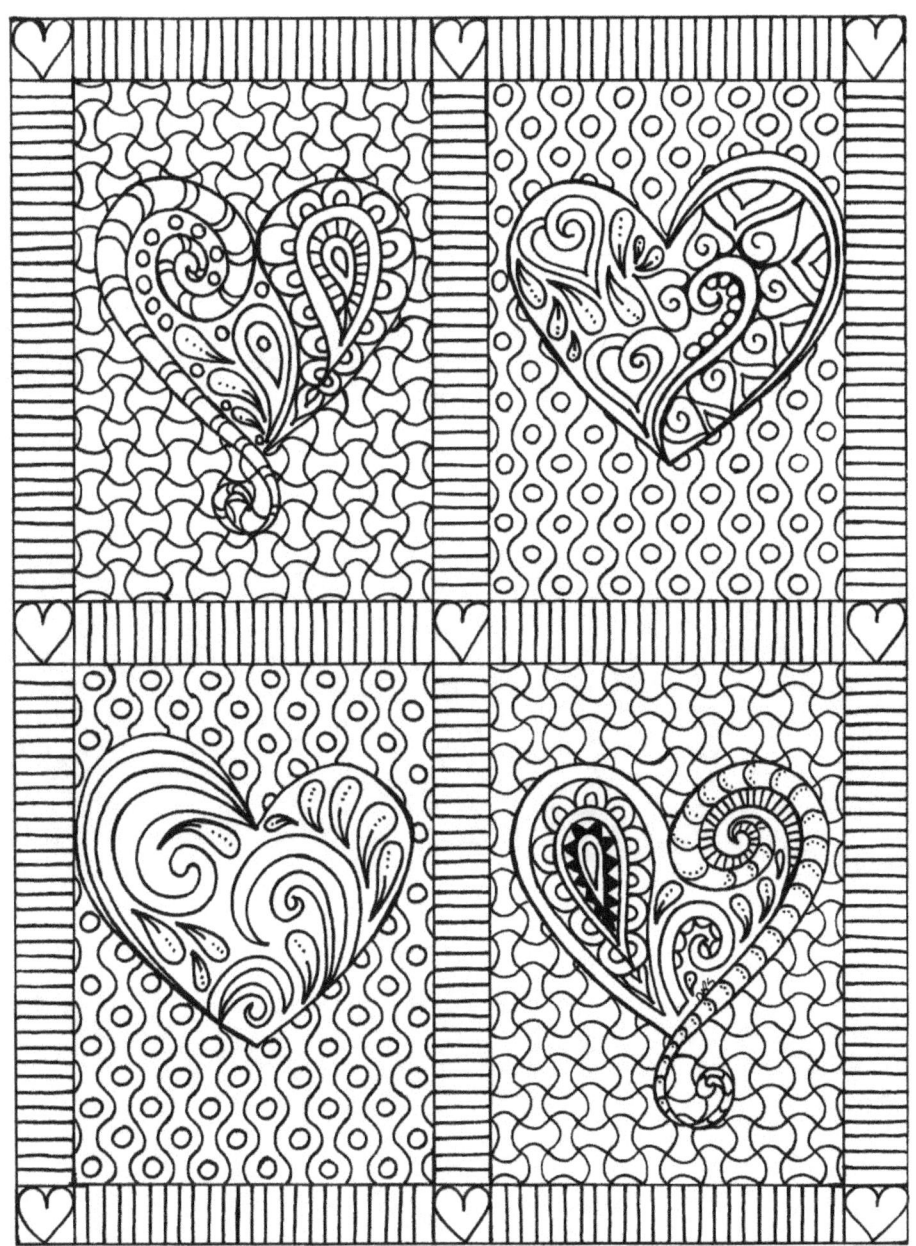

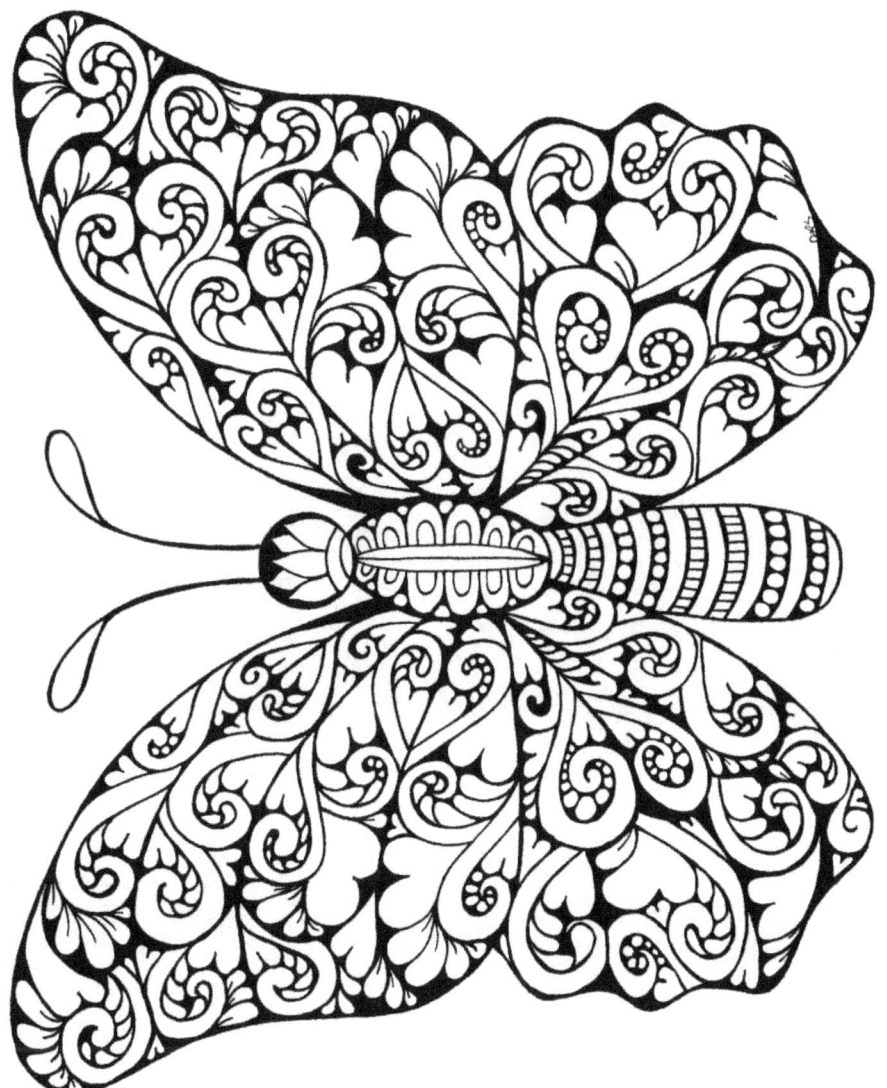

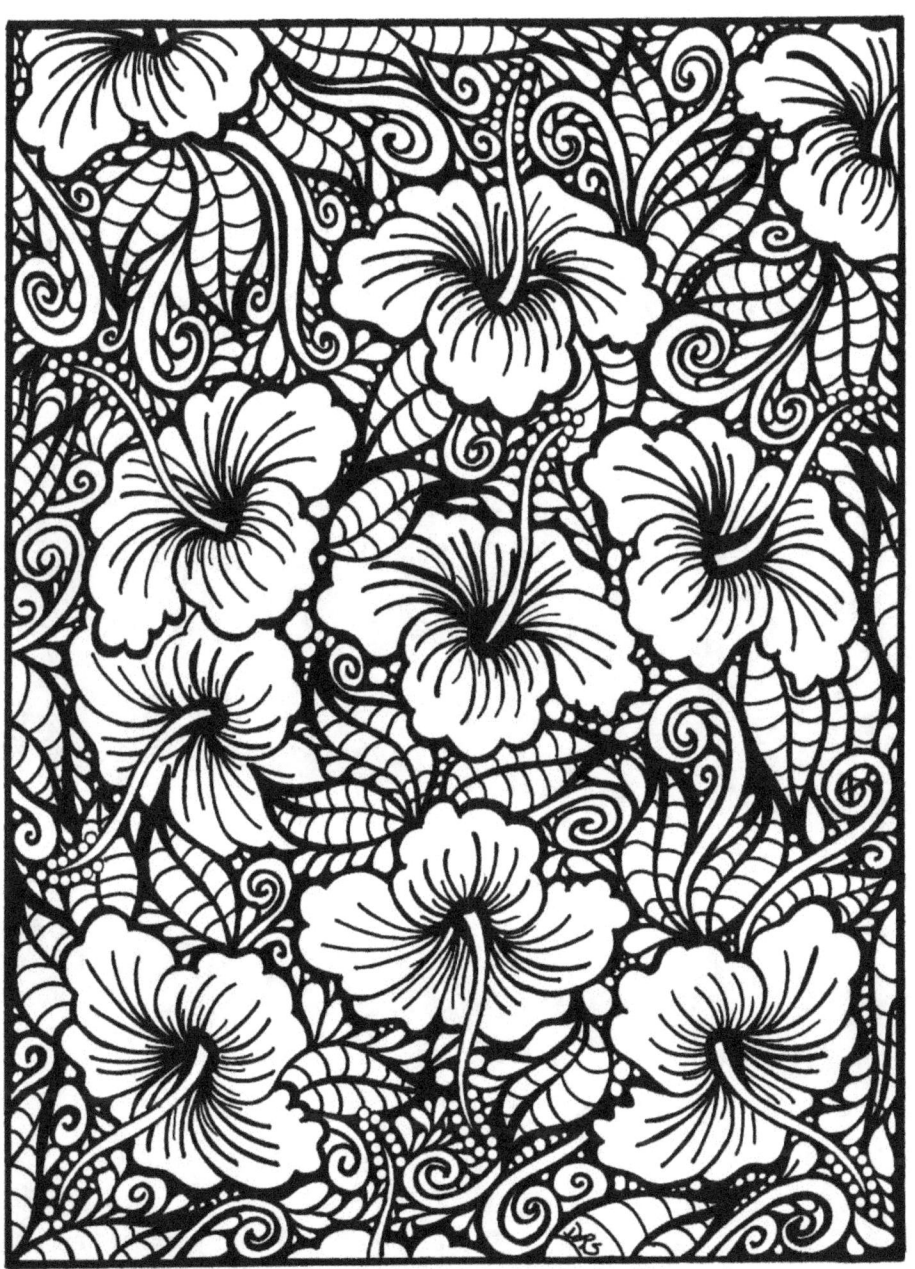

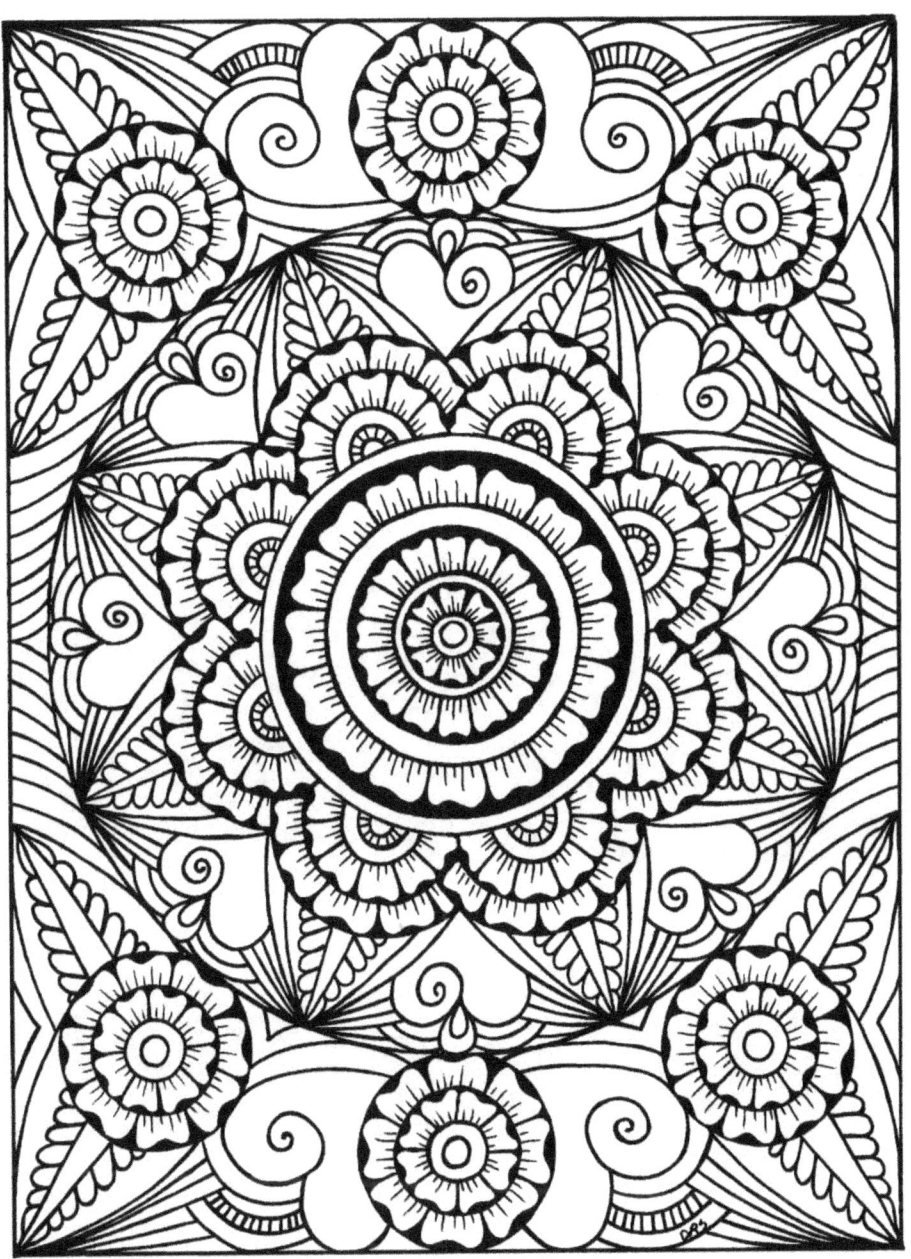

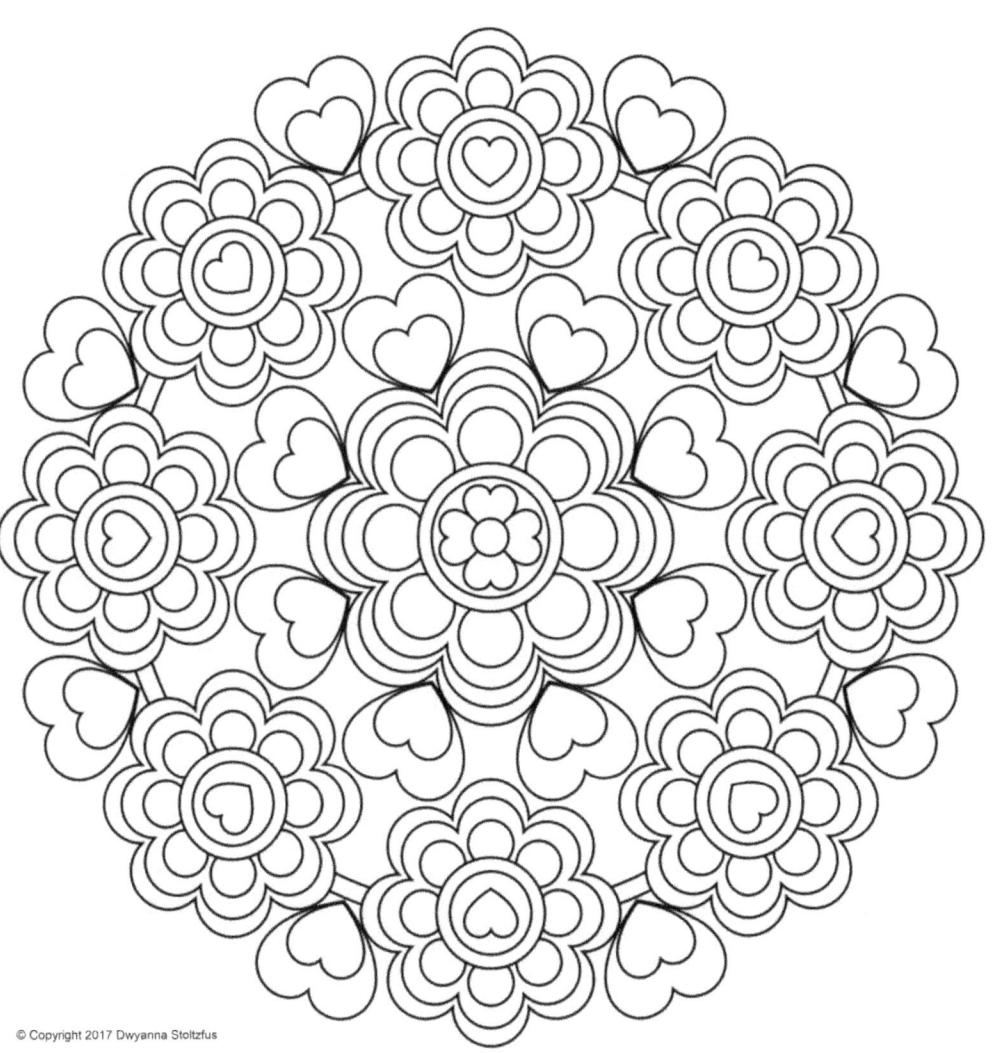

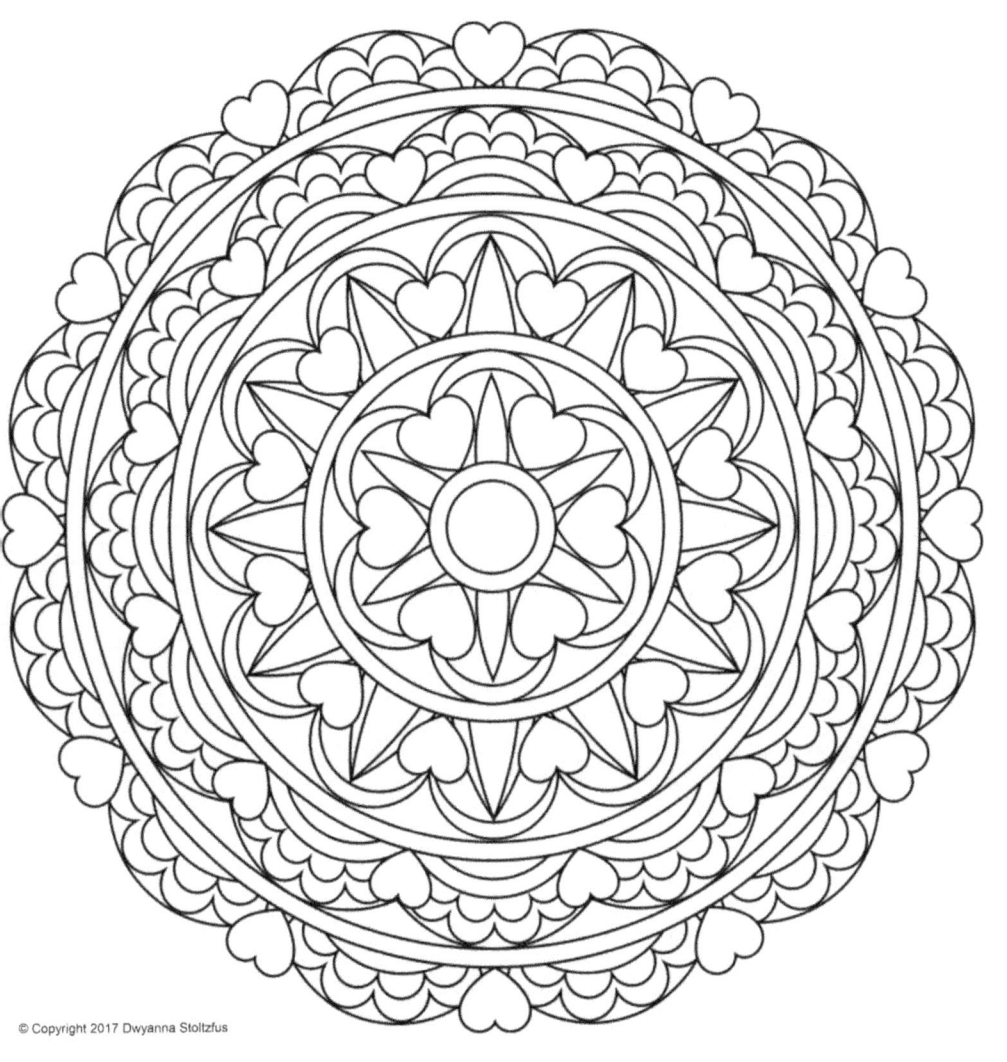

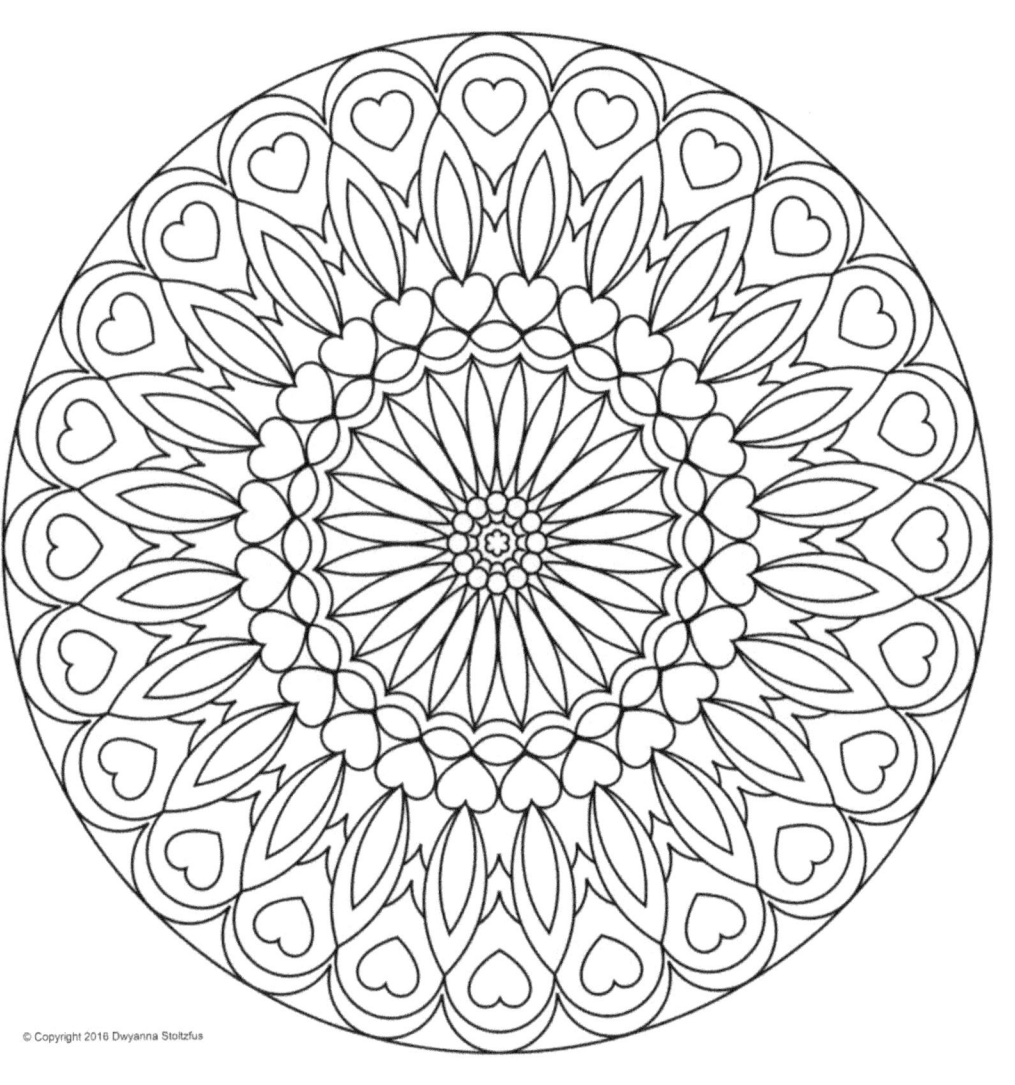

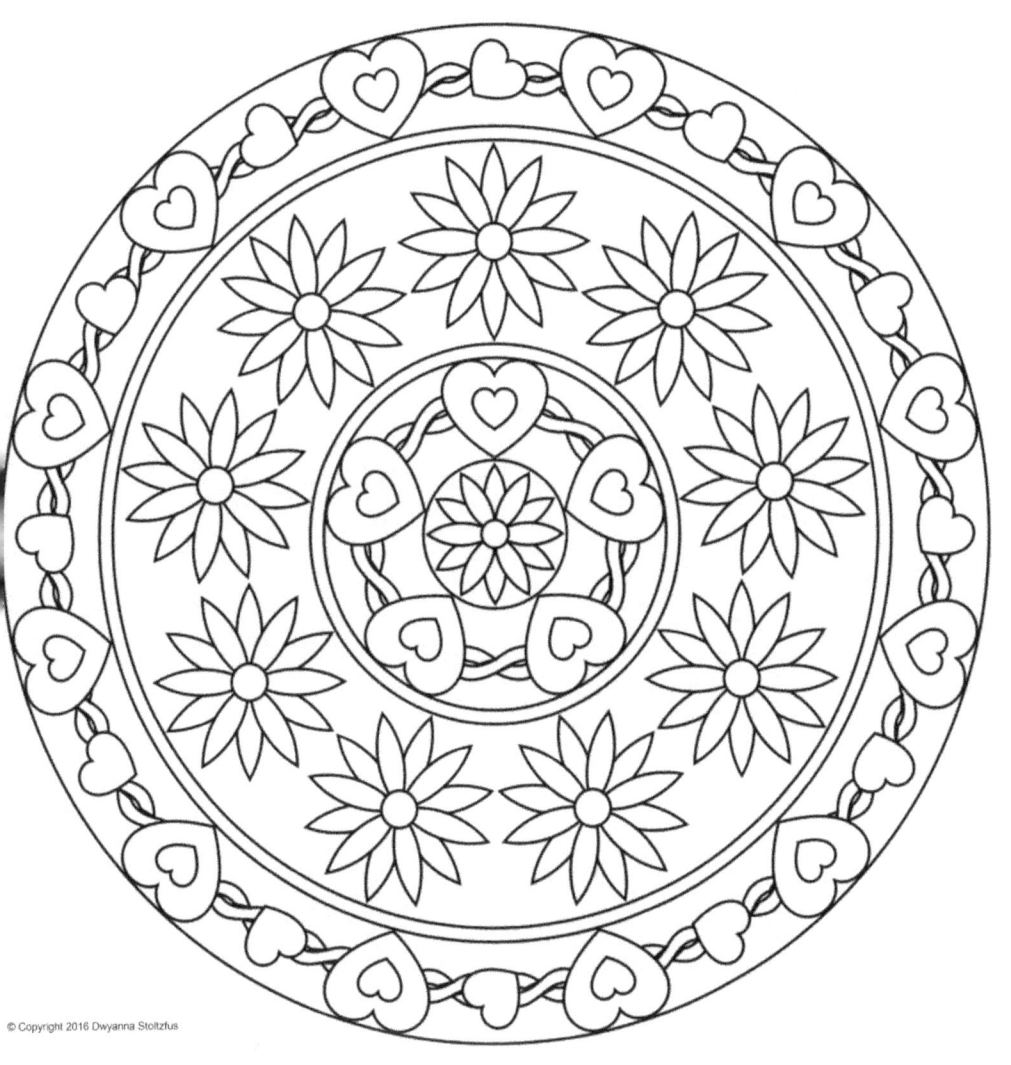

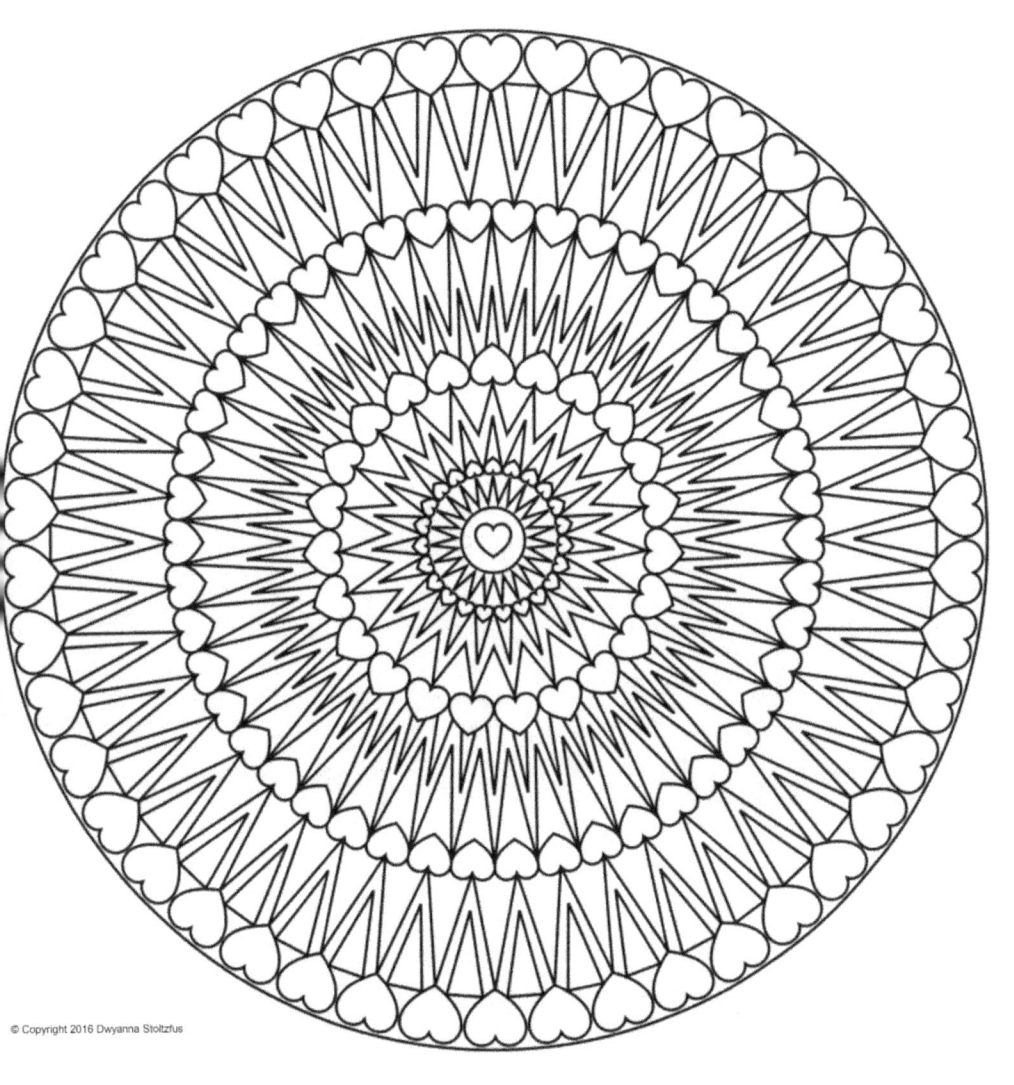

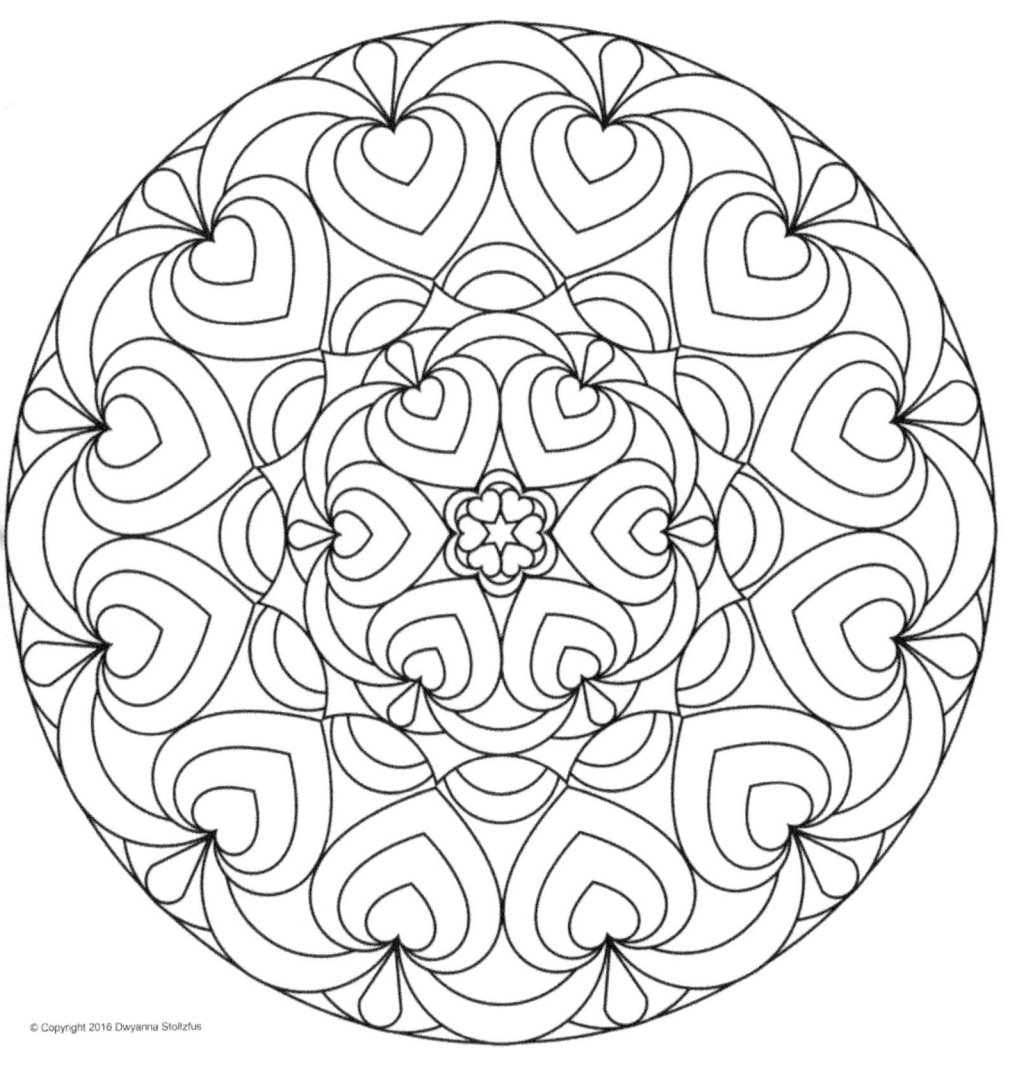

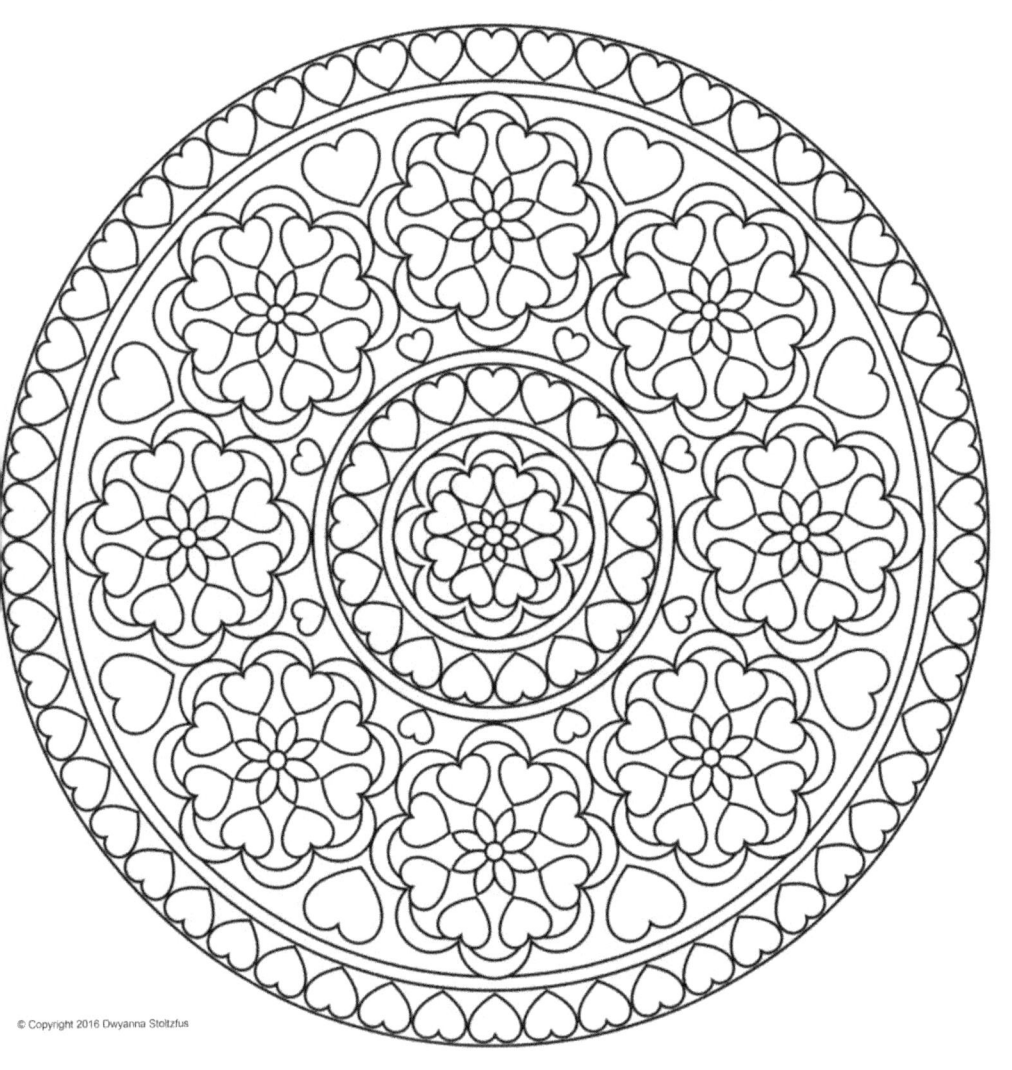

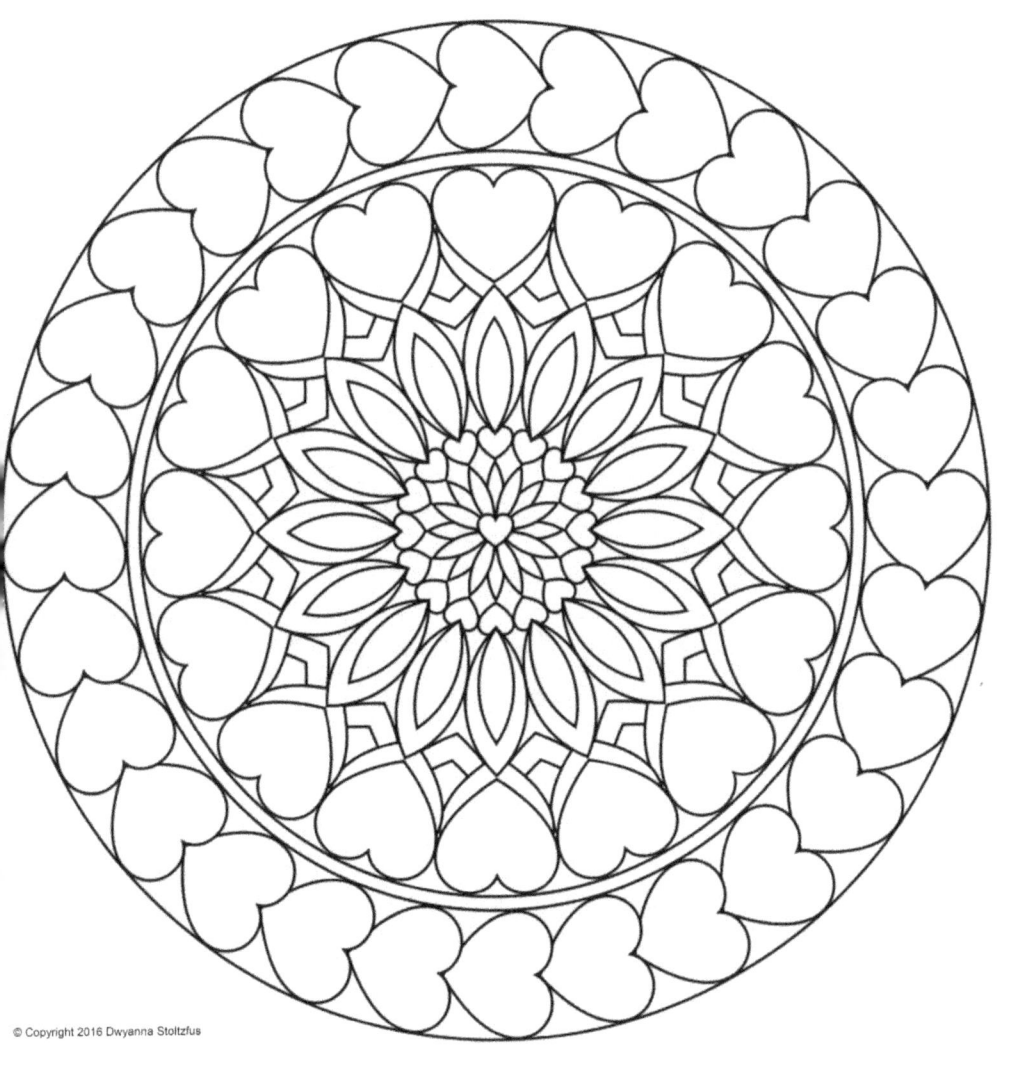

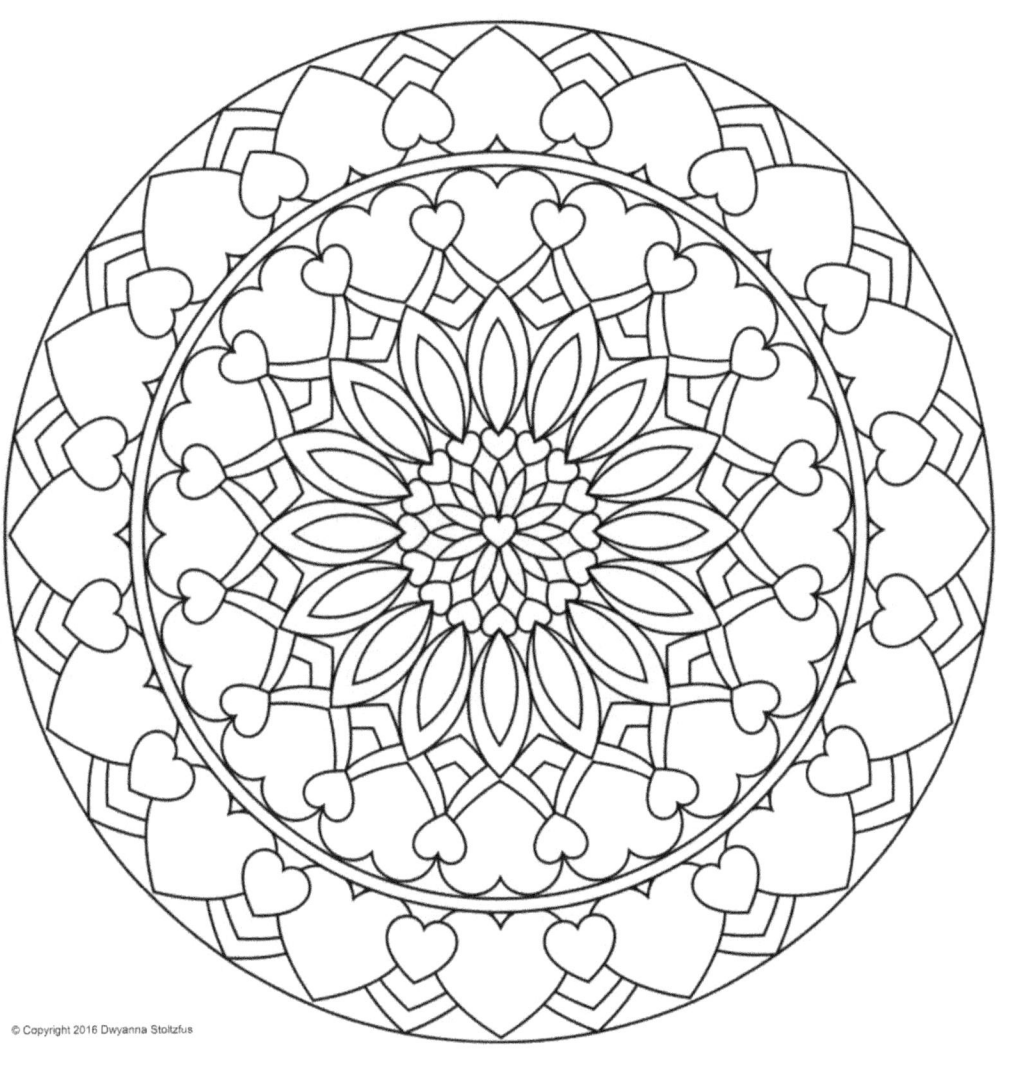

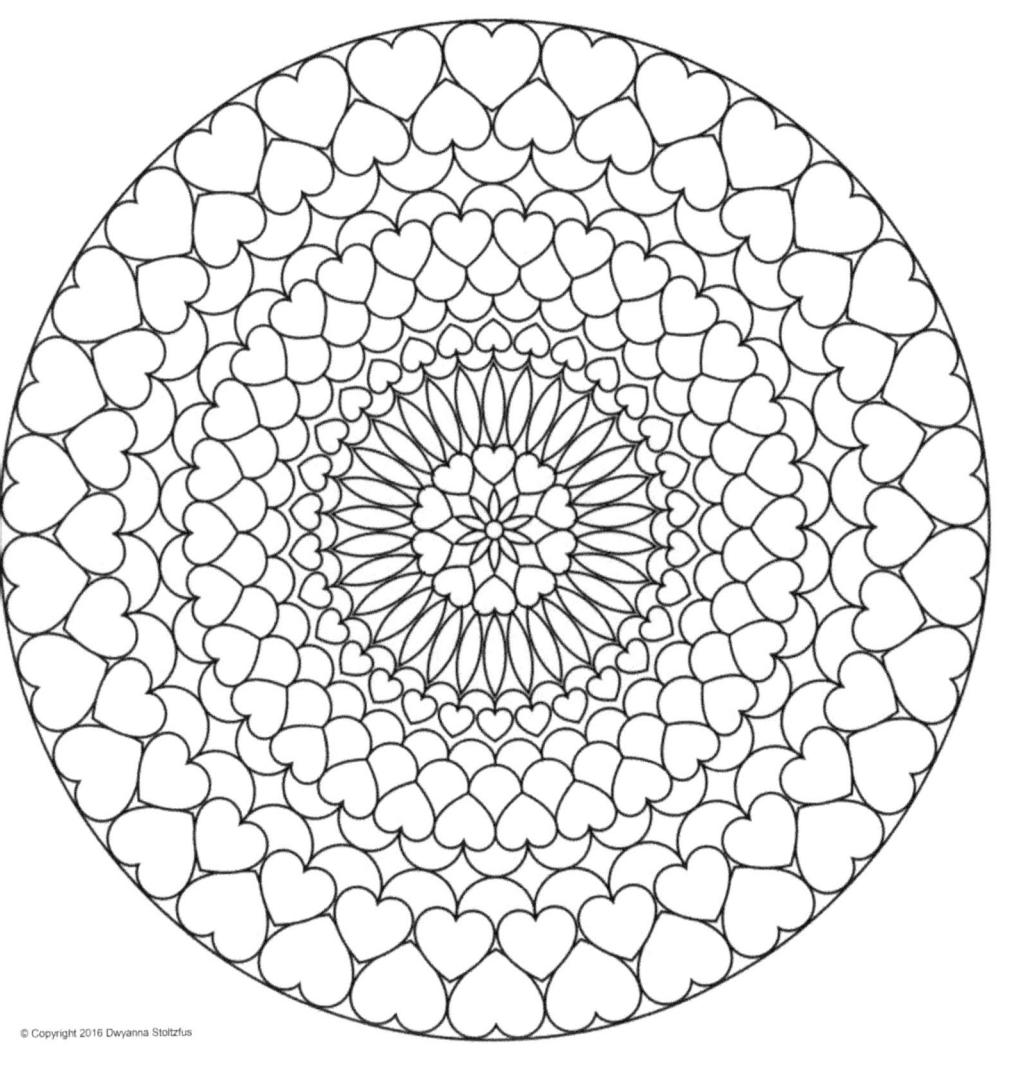

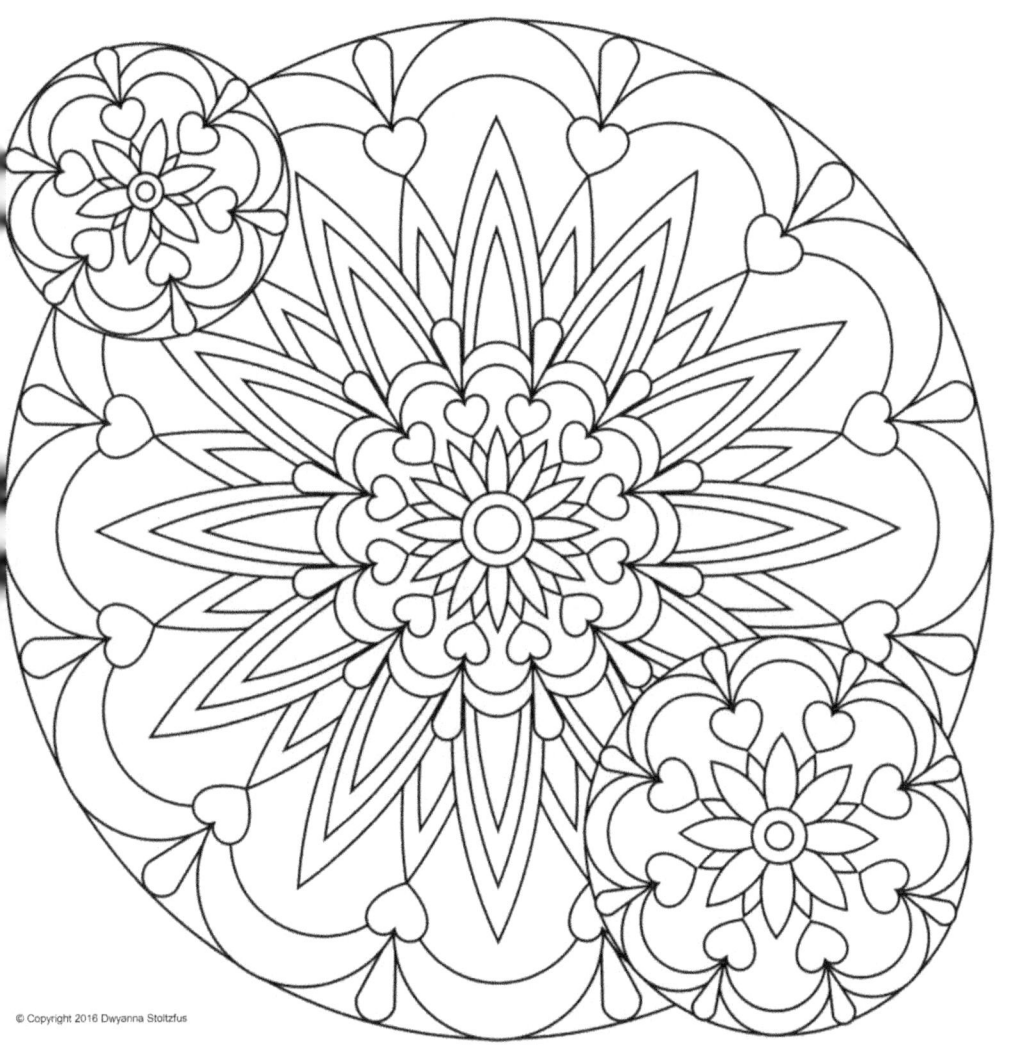

www.ingramcontent.com/pod-product-compliance
Lightning Source LLC
Chambersburg PA
CBHW071753170526
45167CB00003B/1012